CONVICTIONS

CONVICTIONS

POLITICAL PRISONERS—
THEIR STORIES

Arthur Dobrin
Lyn Dobrin
Thomas F. Liotti

ORBIS  BOOKS

Maryknoll, New York 10545

The Catholic Foreign Mission Society of America (Maryknoll) recruits and trains people for overseas missionary service. Through Orbis Books Maryknoll aims to foster the international dialogue that is essential to mission. The books published, however, reflect the opinions of their authors and are not meant to represent the official position of the society.

Library of Congress Cataloging in Publication Data

Dobrin, Arthur, 1943-
  Convictions.

    1. Civil rights—Case studies. I. Dobrin, Lyn.
II. Liotti, Thomas F. III. Title.
JC571.D62   323.4'092'6   81-2787
ISBN 0-88344-089-X (pbk.)   AACR2

Contents

Brothers, write down everything you see and hear. Keep a record of it all.

Simon Dubnow, 1941, in Riga
as he was being taken away by the
German police

Preface

O N A TRAIN TRIP THROUGH MANCHURIA from Harbin to Bei-jing, we conversed with Madame Liu, our Chinese guide. Our topics ranged from popular American culture to Marxist theory to the Cultural Revolution and how it had affected her in particular.

She explained that, in the beginning, she supported the great Maoist experiment in egalitarianism. To this day she still believes that many of its precepts were correct. But she learned firsthand about some of its excesses.

Madame Liu and her husband were longtime party cadre who had spent their entire adult years working for the government in the cities. With the Cultural Revolution came an emphasis upon eliminating the gap between the peasants and urban intelligentsia. The couple was sent to a May 7 school, an institution created in the countryside where city bureaucrats would have an opportunity for manual labor side by side with workers and peasants. They gladly went, supporting the concept as an important one for a thoroughly revolutionary China.

They were to attend the May 7 school for one month. However, they were asked to stay longer. Months later they realized that most of their associates from the city were also at the school. Furthermore, no one left. The May 7 school had become a detention center for disgraced bureaucrats, meaning nearly everyone with an education in a responsible position.

No one told Madame Liu and her husband that they were detained; there was no barbed wire, there were no armed guards. No charges were brought against them, and, of course, there had been no trial. They lived at the school for nearly a year before the atmosphere in the nation changed once again and the force of the Cultural Revolution began to wane. One day they simply packed their bags and left.

This story illustrates the difficulty in defining what a political prisoner is. Clearly, the couple went to the May 7 school for ideological and political reasons. What is not so clear is whether or not they were prisoners. Can a place without bars or walls, a place without physical punishment or jailers, a place where no one is told they must stay, be considered a prison?

Similar kinds of problems arise in other countries, as the following anecdotes demonstrate.

We visited with the late Allard Lowenstein, who at that time served as America's special ambassador for human rights at the United Nations. Lowenstein, a liberal activist most noted for his successful efforts to prevent Lyndon Johnson's running for a second term as president, worked with Andrew Young, the outspoken and sometimes brash ambassador appointed by President Carter.

As private citizens, we went to see Lowenstein to express our concern about several Americans who had been designated by Amnesty International as political prisoners. Lowenstein listened sympathetically, until we used the term "political prisoner." His temper flared and he lectured us about our loose terminology. There were miscarriages of justice in the United States, he said. As a civil rights activist he knew that. But, he said, that is not to say that America has political prisoners. According to Lowenstein, there were no political prisoners in America's prisons.

Less than a year later, Ambassador Young caused a storm of controversy in the United States when, in an interview with a French newspaper, he alleged that there were perhaps thousands of political prisoners in the United States. No one else in the administration publicly backed his charges. For this and other indiscretions Young was replaced by a more temperate successor.

During the 1980 summer Olympics in Moscow, a group of French athletes met with two top Soviet officials to deliver an appeal calling for noninterference in other countries and the liberation of Soviets imprisoned for their "opinions or ideas." After the meeting, which was described as frank and friendly, Vladimir Popov, first deputy chief of the Moscow Olympic Organizing Committee, said that he could agree with the athletes on most points.

But, he said, "There is one paragraph, which we can't agree with them about, that deals with the request to liberate prisoners arrested for expressing thoughts or views. We explained that, in accord with the Soviet constitution and laws currently in effect, we have no political prisoners in this country. If there are prisoners, they are, as in any civilized state, in custody for their criminal actions."

Popov was technically correct. Soviet prisoners are charged and tried. They are duly sentenced by proper authorities. The problem is what is considered criminal. In the Soviet Union, spreading false statements regarding the nature of the Soviet system is considered illegal. All speech or writing deemed anti-Soviet propaganda is seen as similar to shouting fire in a crowded theater; the words are of such a nature as to create a clear and present danger and are no longer protected under the constitutional provisions.

Even if agreement could be reached concerning terminology, there is another dilemma. Disagreement can arise over whether human rights can or should apply universally.

Ethical relativism claims that to argue that something is good is no more than to utter a preference. The good is not objective but subjectively determined. Ethical choices are therefore merely matters of taste, with no rational basis for selecting between options. This means that two governments might reach opposing conclusions regarding the desirability of granting human rights. Ethical relativism holds that if one government contends that human rights are a good and another nation holds that genocide is a good there is no way of selecting between these arguments objectively. Whatever is claimed to be good is good.

Allied with this position is cultural relativism. Each culture has its own standards of right and wrong and the only test of correctness is the internal consistency which a culture exhibits. In one place polygamy is outlawed, in another it is the norm.

From either perspective—philosophical or cultural relativism—it follows that there is no universal standard of ethical behavior. In this way, human rights cannot be universally upheld in theory.

In fact, while these kinds of objections are often voiced by critics of human rights organizations, they are seldom raised in the political arena. The most common form of justification for dissent from a human rights position is the argument appealing to mitigating circumstances. A Kenyan official articulated this in a conversation when he noted that his country was too young and fragile, had too many serious problems to overcome, and was too lacking in an informed citizenry able to discriminate between constructive and destructive criticism to allow "rumor mongers" to sow discord.

"You can afford to tolerate dissension," he said. "We are too weak for it."

This justification was echoed by the Israeli government in response to an Amnesty International report. The report appealed to the Israelis to establish a public and impartial inquiry to investigate complaints of brutality to people arrested on suspicion of security offenses in Occupied Territories. Attorney General Itzhak Zamir responded by saying that Israel faced an "exceptional dilemma." He noted, "In these circumstances, the question of human rights takes on a very different complexion."

Both the Kenyan and Israeli positions acknowledge human rights as a correct goal but argue that neither country can implement these rights fully at this time. This response reflects the growing recognition of human rights as a universal good. It is a rare government that will attack the idea of human rights per se.

Governments have grown increasingly sensitive to world opinion on this matter. Few nations want to be perceived as brutally disregarding fundamental rights. Most often when human rights have been abrogated, the government attempts to justify its action by claiming mitigating circumstances. Not one United Nations member objects to the inclusion of the Universal Declaration of Human Rights as part of the U.N. charter. Those countries that have not signed the Covenant regarding human rights, such as the United States, do so not out of objection to the stated principles but because of the finer legal point regarding the authority of the enforcing agency.

Nations want to present an image of decency and concern for human welfare. Few want to admit to having political prisoners. Consequently, means of political repression that present to the world a cleaner image are becoming common. Some nations fabricate criminal charges and produce bogus evidence to convict dissidents; others define certain acts of dissidence as criminal. Other countries claim a state of emergency and "temporarily" suspend liberties such as free speech and assembly. House arrests, banning orders, "disappearances," and repeated short-term arrests and harassment are common features in several countries.

One can take heart by the verbal agreement given to the concept of human rights by nearly every nation throughout the world. But as the plight of the world's hundreds of thousands of political prisoners illustrates, there is a chasm between human rights rhetoric and reality.

Acknowledgments

Hans Gunzenhauser, for his translations from German; Laurie Wiseberg of Human Rights Internet; Ramon Hodel and Larry Cox of Amnesty International; Sylvia Kaufman, for her research assistance.

Diana Houstoun
and
Elisabeth Kasemann

Argentina

Everyone has the right to freedom of thought, conscience and religion; this right includes freedom to change his religion or belief, and freedom, either alone or in community with others, and in public or private, to manifest his religion or belief in teaching, practice, worship and observance.

Article 18, Universal Declaration
of Human Rights

Argentina's history has been one of weak civilian governments and a strong military. Prior to the military coup in 1966, Argentina experienced five different presidents—three civilian and two military—in eleven years. While the military government attempted to bring economic order to the country, unemployment continued to grow. An uprising in the city of Córdoba in 1969 led to twenty civilian deaths and a declaration of a state of siege.

1

The military consented to elections in 1973. But the new civilian government was unable to control either terrorism or inflation. By early 1974, over half of the 6,000 Americans in Argentina fled, fearful of their safety. By early 1976, inflation reached an annual rate of 700 percent.

On March 24, 1976, the military seized power again, promising to restore economic stability and to wage war against left-wing subversives. In a widely-cited comment attributed to him shortly after the coup, General Benjamin Menéndez is reported to have said, "We are going to have to kill 50,000 people: 25,000 subversives; 20,000 sympathizers; and we will make 5,000 mistakes."

It is not clear whether the Argentine government considered Diana Houstoun and her friend Elisabeth Kasemann sympathizers, subversives, or mistakes.

O N WEDNESDAY MORNING, March 9, 1977, Elisabeth Kasemann failed to show up for an appointment with her friend Diana Houstoun in Diana's apartment in Buenos Aires. Because the appointment was for an early hour Diana did not give the matter much thought. By evening she was worried.

"On Thursday I began to move like nobody's business," Diana explains. "When a friend doesn't appear for a day, you don't think she's been hit by a car and is hospitalized. Because of what's happened to other people you think, 'They've got her.' I called people up to contact her father, a prominent German theologian."

By "they" Diana meant the police. Both she and Elisabeth had reason to fear police interest in their activities. The two were active in student, labor, and political work considered subversive by the Argentine government; they had helped people escape from the country. Both had become politically aware; then, through experience at Union Theological Seminary in Buenos Aires, they became critics of the Argentine government.

Thursday evening when Diana returned from work, the night porter stopped her as she entered the lobby. "The police were here today looking for you," he told her. "They were here this afternoon."

He asked her not to tell anyone that he had informed her about the police visit. He feared for his own security. She went to her apartment. Nothing had been touched.

"They never come to arrest you during the day. It's all done between midnight and the early hours of morning. I had a choice then. I could turn on my heel and run for it. But I heard of too many friends that had been killed that way."

Public policy in this regard was clearly spelled out. Article 5 of Decree 21.264, issued on March 24, 1976, authorized security forces to use weapons when a person *"in flagrante delicto . . .* does not cease upon first warning or uses arms against the officer of the peace."

"I knew that if the police had already been to my apartment they were watching. I think that it was a reasonable guess that there were people outside, and if I tried to run I would have gotten shot."

She spent the night disposing of books and other items that might be considered incriminating evidence. She tore pages from books and from her address book and flushed them down the toilet. She phoned her office to inform them of the impending danger. She gave them her ID number and passport number.

"I didn't go to bed because I knew that they were going to come. But I put on a dressing gown and dozed on a chair. I wasn't going to run because that would be to incriminate myself. One always has this naive feeling that 'I'm not guilty of anything,' which is the way I felt. I was guilty of not being a fascist, but that's all I was guilty of." The police arrived at midnight. They surrounded the entire block and four trucks full of armed men in civilian dress waited. Her neighbors were put into the elevator to prevent them from witnessing the arrest.

"All of a sudden the doors blew in. I only got a chance to see boots and guns before they threw me to the floor and blindfolded me. They beat me across the head with something soft. I don't know what it was. All I could hear around me was things breaking. Furniture. Guns cracking. It's really intimidating because you can't see it. Once they cut off your senses you really begin to feel terrified."

They repeatedly asked her name. They asked her what she did in 1973, why she went to Chile, who her friends were, what work she did.

"Where are her belongings?" one of the soldiers asked her. Diana knew immediately that her arrest was connected to Elisabeth's disappearance.

"They took me into the bedroom and started beating me up,

and they said I better tell them the truth because they had methods for getting the truth out of me. They were going through my papers, and I could hear the banging and crashing going on."

The police told her that she had a lot of subversive literature. They were referring to her books from the seminary, including *Marx and the Bible.*

They took Diana to a waiting car. The police changed her blindfold to a thick elastic band which cut into her face and muffled her hearing.

"Don't touch your blindfold," a guard warned her. "It's your life insurance."

She understood his comment. "If one of the top officers decides that you're going to be released, they don't want you coming after them later. That's one explanation for the blindfold. The other is intimidation."

They drove her around about a half hour. By this time she had begun to compose herself and remember some of the rules she and her friends had discussed in case of an arrest. "One of the things to do is memorize the time so you have an idea where they're taking you. I didn't have any idea where we were going, but I did try to keep track of the time."

When they arrived at their destination, they took Diana from the car and put shackles with two padlocks around her legs. "You no longer have a name," someone said to her. "You are now F-39." She was taken to a room where she could hear typing. They removed her watch.

"Would you like some water?"

That's when Diana became terrified. She remembered another rule her companions had worked out: Don't drink water.

"Offering water is a symbol of what's to come. They always give water before they use electric shock on you." Water in the body serves as a conductor for the electricity. She refused the water.

They took her across the room, banged on a door, and took her down a staircase. This was the torture area.

"I heard people screaming. I thought I heard Elisabeth screaming. I don't know if I really did. It may sound sadistic but I was hoping that I wasn't there alone. That's partly what pulls you through, feeling as a prisoner that you are not alone, that there is a community of you. The moment you're isolated, I think you've had it."

They took off her dressing gown. She was naked except for the blindfold and chains.

They questioned her for the next nine hours, constantly threatening to use electric shock. Diana remembered another rule: Don't say anything significant for the first twenty-four hours if at all possible. "If you have any friends who might be suspicious and whom they want to arrest, you give them time to disappear."

The interrogators threatened Diana with the arrest of her family. "Do you have a six-year-old niece? We're bringing her in any time now."

They threatened her with torture.

"Do you hear the screams? You'll be screaming worse than that in a while."

They hit her on the head and punched her in the abdomen.

"Do you know Elisabeth Kasemann? Do you trust her?"

"Yes, very much. She has the keys to my apartment."

"That's not true," someone said and beat her again. An interrogator left the room and returned quickly. "Yes, it's true," he said.

Diana was convinced that Elisabeth was being held next door and the interrogator had checked Diana's statement with her. Although Diana never saw her, she is certain that Elisabeth was being tortured.

The police threatened to torture Diana again. They ran a piece of iron up and down her chest saying, "This is going to get hot."

They asked her more questions. "What do you think of the Third World, the peace movement, the Vatican Council, the National Council of Churches?" They asked about her work and she gave answers that she knew would not harm anyone. When they asked for names, she gave them only the names of work colleagues, names they already knew.

Because of the questions being asked and the questions that were not asked, Diana knew that the police still knew nothing about the people she had been helping to leave Argentina. This meant that Elisabeth had not spoken either. This gave Diana more courage to resist.

"What do you think of Jews?" they asked.

She responded the way she had to many questions before—dull, feigning stupidity. "I don't know any Jews. I can't give you an opinion about them."

Two of Diana's closest friends were Jews, but she knew that to say that would have brought on another beating.

Her interrogators responded with a diatribe against the Jews. This got Diana so angry that she blurted out, "Are you Christians?"

The room was silent. Then one of the interrogators laughed and placed Diana's hand on his chest. She fingered a metal swastika. Another grabbed her hand and put it on a cross he was wearing. "We're good Catholics." She was beaten again.

The interrogators left the room for five minutes. One returned and said, "If you face the wall, I'll take your blindfold off for a minute."

Diana's anger had altered the situation. "Something had changed. They treat you like an object and you respond like an object. Now I was more responsive. I pulled myself together. It was a sign that something had broken. I felt more confident."

Diana could hear prisoners shuffling through the corridor with shackles on their legs. She also heard her interrogators talking about whether or not to burn her. A short while later someone came back.

"We're taking you out. We're going to take you back to your apartment and see who comes to visit."

Diana is uncertain why she was not given electric shock. "I received better treatment than I've heard anyone receiving. Maybe they knew that they were dealing with a British citizen. Maybe it's because they knew I wasn't a guerilla."

She was blindfolded again and led upstairs. They removed the chains, gave back her dressing gown, threw her in the back of a car, and drove her home.

Four soldiers, in civilian clothes, took her to her apartment. They claimed to be officers and said that they had not slept for three days. When they arrived at her apartment, they took her blindfold off.

"I was shocked to see the apartment. They had dismantled the whole thing when they arrested me. They left nothing, not even my clothes. Everything was gone except a table, a record player, kitchen utensils, and a Hebrew Bible. Otherwise nothing was left. There was hardly anything there to prove that I had ever lived there. It was demoralizing. I felt like nobody again."

Diana was allowed to drink water and use the toilet. For the next two days they tormented her. The four officers took turns sleeping and raping her.

On Sunday night they told her that she was under house arrest. "Tomorrow you are to go to work as if nothing has happened."

"How can I do that? I don't have my ID card. Unless you're crazy you don't go out on the streets without your ID."

"Tough luck. But that's what you're going to do."

"I need some clothes, some money."

They gave her permission to call her sister after they were gone.

"You have to leave the country. We'll return your passports. But don't do anything foolish. Until you leave there will be someone with you all the time."

They left. Diana's sister brought her food, money, and clothes.

"Don't stay here," Diana told her. "Get the hell out."

That was the last night she spent in her apartment. From then on she slept on the floor of her office.

Although she never saw anyone on the streets whom she suspected of following her, she felt as though she were constantly being watched. Each afternoon she reported to a police officer in a downtown cafeteria. He returned both her Argentine and British passports and granted her permission to visit her parents one weekend.

"Remember, when you leave, the law has a long arm. You have family and friends here," the officer warned her.

One day Diana received a call from Elisabeth's father in Germany. "She's sick," Diana said. "Very sick. Get a doctor."

When she reported to the officer the next day, he told her he knew about her conversation with Dr. Kasemann.

This continued for two weeks. The day before leaving, Diana asked the officer what they had against Elisabeth.

"Nothing much," he said. "Only ideology."

On April 4 she left Argentina, stopped in Peru for two days, then arrived in New York. She spent the next ten days convalescing.

At the airport in Lima, Peru, Diana met with a lawyer, a friend

of Dr. Kasemann. He took a statement from her and flew with it
to Germany. While Elisabeth's case became a major news item in
Germany, the Bonn government acted slowly. At first they did not
believe the story; then they offered a mild criticism of the Argentine government. Dr. Kasemann was frustrated. "Humanity as
well as democracy are . . . administered bureaucratically, and the
sale of a Mercedes weighs more than a human life," he said in an
interview with the *Frankfurt Rundschau* in August.

A cable from the German Embassy in Madrid to Buenos Aires
requesting information on Elisabeth's whereabouts produced a
reply eight days later stating that the Argentine government had
never heard of Elisabeth Kasemann.

On May 26, Argentine dailies reported a shoot-out between
guerrilla groups and government agents in the town of Monte
Grande two days earlier. On May 30, a casualty list was issued:
sixteen guerillas dead, including a woman of unknown national-
ity, known as Isabella or Christine Kasermann. The government
claimed that a leadership conference of five extreme left groups
took place to create a united front, and that Isabella Kasermann
participated in the conference as a representative of one of the
groups.

June 4. Isabella is identified as Elisabeth Kasemann, daughter
of Professor Dr. Ernst Kasemann of Germany.

June 6. The Kasemann family receives official notice of their
daughter's death.

June 8. A death certificate is issued.

Under mounting pressure by groups in Germany, the Bonn government requested that the Argentine government return the
body to Tübingen. On June 12, the Institute for Forensic Medi-
cine at the University of Tübingen performed a post mortem.
Their report concluded that Elisabeth Kasemann was shot in the
back by an automatic weapon and three times in the area of the
neck and heart. Her body showed signs of torture.

Said Dr. Kasemann upon hearing the report, "This is the way
executions are done."

The Argentine government has not altered its story about the
alleged shoot-out in Monte Grande. But according to information released by Amnesty International's Argentina Coordination
Group in Tübingen, Germany, almost a year after Elisabeth's de-

tention she had been imprisoned in Barracks 1 of the Army Command Palmero, probably the same place at which Diana was questioned. She was tortured so severely that she became ill and needed to be nursed back to health by fellow prisoners. Two attempts were made to negotiate a ransom for her release. Reliable sources, whose identity Amnesty International will not reveal for fear of reprisals, claim that a $25,000 ransom was discussed.

A report prepared by the Inter-American Human Rights Commission in mid-1979 confirms that what happened to Diana and Elisabeth was not an isolated incident. The preliminary report presented to the General Assembly of the Organization of American States cited evidence of methodical killing and torture of prisoners in recent years. While the report notes that there has been an effort by the military government to reduce human rights violations, according to the government's own figures there are still 1,438 prisoners held under the state of siege. At least 1,500 other persons have been tried and sentenced by military courts.

Recently Dr. Kasemann wrote, "My point is not to seek revenge for my daughter. I do not want to envision and defend her as a martyr. However, I would like her death to open people's eyes so that the reality of Argentina, so beautiful and yet harboring an inferno, can be seen. I should not like to leave the last word to the executioners and the military."

Diana Houstoun, who now lives in New York City and attends Union Theological Seminary, also does not wish to leave the last word to the executioners.

"When it comes down to dealing with critical situations of life and death, what holds it together is loving other people and believing that you are not alone. You read in the Gospels that Christ says that there is no greater love than for a person to lay down his life for his friends. That's exactly what it's come to. If you can feel that it is true, that there are people really caring and loving that way, it makes a big difference. God is a living presence, a living faith."

Yuri Handler

Soviet Union

Everyone has the right to freedom of opinion and expression; this right includes freedom to hold opinions without interference and to seek, receive and impart information and ideas through any media and regardless of frontiers.

Article 19, Universal Declaration of Human Rights

Three years after Stalin's death, Nikita Khrushchev denounced the Soviet Union's former leader at a secret session of the Twentieth Party Congress. The year 1956 was the peak of post-Stalin liberalization with the en masse release of prisoners from labor camps and the formal clearing of many disgraced intellectuals of charges leveled against them during the Stalin period. Literary committees were established to publish or re-issue the works of Soviet writers whose works had formerly been forbidden.

With the Hungarian uprising in October, however, the more conservative forces in the government asserted themselves, establishing a hiatus in liberalizing policies. But by 1959, with Khrushchev firmly in control, a new wave of cultural liberalization swept the country, reaching its climax in 1962 with the publication of Solzhenitsyn's scathing indictment of the Soviet labor camp system, One Day in the Life of Ivan Denisovich.

After Khrushchev's removal from power, the Soviet Union's attitude toward its writers hardened once more. In 1966, two writers were sentenced to long prison terms for publishing works abroad under pen names, Solzhenitsyn could not find a publisher for his latest work, and censorship controls were tightened.

It was in this period that Yuri Handler distributed samizdat *(unpublished works, usually in mimeographed form) and* tamizdat *(published books smuggled into the Soviet Union).*

WESTERN CLASSICS, such as *Treasure Island*, touched something deep in Yuri Handler that prescribed Soviet literature left cold. He had no room in his soul for what he saw as the dull and pervasive Marxist philosophy. Yuri did not reject Marxism; it always was foreign to his psyche.

His love for books eventually led to Modrovia labor camp.

Yuri was still in law school when Boris Pasternak, after unsuccessful efforts to find a Soviet publisher, turned to an Italian firm to print *Doctor Zhivago*. Pasternak won the Nobel Prize for literature in 1958 but came under the opprobrium of Soviet officials. *Doctor Zhivago* became a best-seller in the West, yet copies were not made available within Russia. The book was not officially banned—there is no index or censorship—but for all practical purposes possession of the book was prohibited.

For Yuri and others like him, Pasternak stood as a symbol of peaceful and subtle resistance against the existing order.

In 1962 Yuri began distributing copies of Pasternak's novel in *samizdat*. He gave out copies of the book for aesthetic reasons rather than as an act of political defiance, although in the view of the Marxist government, literature and politics cannot be separated, and therefore Yuri's action, by definition, was political.

"I understood that there was danger involved. But everything is dangerous. You couldn't live in a world if you thought about everything in terms of danger. I understood the possible consequences of my action. I expected someday that I would be arrested. But I couldn't do otherwise."

Soviet authorities seemed to be unaware of Yuri's activities until 1965. At that time he came into contact with a group which referred to itself as Real Marxists. Yuri did not join them because he rejected Marxism in every form, yet he felt sympathetic toward them to the extent that he shared their dislike of the nation as it was then constituted. Both he and the Real Marxists condemned Soviet bureaucracy.

Yuri provided the group with several books that could not be obtained through legitimate channels, including one written by a Yugoslav critical of Marxist practices in that country. When the Soviets uncovered the existence of the underground Real Marxists and arrested its members, they found Milovan Djilas's *New Class* and traced the book back to Yuri.

The KGB demanded that Yuri surrender all of his unauthorized political books.

"I had a little daughter, Paullina, my first child. I was really in love with her. At that time I wasn't prepared to go to prison, so I gave up three of the books that I had."

Yuri kept other books and the KGB did not search his apartment.

At first, the fear of imprisonment prevented Yuri from disseminating literature. But within six months his concern for aesthetics and free thought asserted itself once more.

"I didn't stop because I believed so strongly that what I was doing was the correct thing. Eventually I engaged in book distribution again."

Yuri's work as a legal consultant for a furniture factory in Leningrad often took him to Moscow. In the latter half of 1965 he became acquainted with the incipient human rights movement. Members of this movement tried to dissuade Yuri from book distribution because they felt that the government would find those actions illegal under the Articles of Criminal Code No. 70 which forbade dissemination of anti-Soviet propaganda. They wanted to make the human rights movement an open opposition which would be above legal reproach. Yuri chose to remain on the periphery of the movement.

"What I did, from my point of view, was a normal thing. From the viewpoint of all civilized law, human law and natural law, reading and discussing books is legal."

As Yuri's contacts widened, so did his distribution network. Many Soviets, including several in prominent, official positions, took books from him. During his frequent Moscow visits, Yuri engaged in spontaneous dinner discussions about books with his friends.

In January 1968, Yuri took further action. He wrote a letter to *Pravda, Izvestia,* and several Western leftist newspapers protesting the trial of Aleksandr Ginzburg. Ginzburg was being tried for publishing an unauthorized book about the trial of two Russian writers. Yuri also gave a copy of the letter to a friend in Moscow who passed it on to a Western journalist.

He followed this letter with several others protesting similar trials.

"I believe that from that moment on the KGB made a decision to arrest me."

Twice in the next several months Yuri was summoned to meet with authorities, once at the KGB headquarters in Leningrad and another time at the office of the deputy executive of the Leningrad Communist Party. Both times he was told that the distribution of *samizdat* and letters protesting trials created enemies for the Soviet Union. The Party deputy told Yuri that if he were unhappy with anything, he should talk to the deputy directly. The deputy stressed the importance of not making his protests public.

The KGB tried a different approach. They knew that Yuri, his wife, Albina, and his daughter had one bedroom in a common apartment with nine other families. Apartment occupancy is controlled by the state. The KGB offered Yuri a larger apartment as well as a better job on condition that he discontinue his activities.

Yuri rejected the offers, making explicit his intention to remain a human rights activist.

"I told them that my activities would help make Soviet society better. Injustices worsen the situation, weaken the system. Many injustices were committed in Stalin's time, and I said I wanted to struggle against the return of Stalinism. I argued that the article of the criminal code under which Ginzburg was tried was unconstitutional since the Soviet constitution guarantees freedom of speech."

Yuri was again summoned by the KGB when he demonstrated against the trial of twenty members of the All Russian Social Christian Union for People's Liberation. He provided the Western press with information about the trial. Yuri again presented himself as an anti-Stalinist and pointed to the constitution which provided for the right to demonstrate.

"My private position was different. I was convinced that free speech would ruin Soviet power. The government would be over-come in one day by free discussion; even one hour would be too much. I deliberately struggled for free speech, free information, because I was sure it would bring down Soviet power."

The KGB continued to watch Yuri closely. They put a tail on him, following him everywhere. Two or three men shadowed his every move. Then, in July, the plainclothesmen were no longer present.

"I didn't know it then but I understand now that this was a dangerous sign, for now they began real watching. They stopped their intimidation and began real surveillance. They ceased warning me."

When a road crew began digging up the street in front of Yuri's apartment, Yuri became suspicious. His friends thought he was over-reacting. However, Yuri remained alert, always expecting to be arrested.

On July 30, 1968, Yuri and some friends spent the evening to-gether discussing the Czechoslovakian experiment in liberaliza-tion. They feared that the Soviet Union might intervene militarily. They decided to write a letter of support from the Leningrad group to the Czech intelligentsia in support of liberalization. Ad-ditionally, a letter would be hand-delivered to the Czech ambassa-dor in Moscow, supporting his government's new policy. They could not reach final agreement on the wording, so planned to meet two days later at Yuri's apartment.

"What we didn't know at that time was that the KGB had bugged the apartment and knew everything we planned."

The twelve friends at that meeting called others who they thought would be interested in signing the letter. Since Yuri ex-pected a large turnout that Thursday night he kept the front door open to the apartment house, as well as the doors to his apart-ment. As the group was working on refining the letter to the am-bassador, Yuri heard many footsteps down the corridor.

"How wonderful, I thought. A lot of people wanted to sign the petition. It is difficult to get one person to sign a letter. Now I was glad so many friends were coming to sign."

The elation quickly left Yuri as he realized that they were not footfalls of friends he heard but those of the police, tough and quick. He rushed to close the door to his room, wanting to burn some documents before the police entered, but they pushed their way in. The police searched the apartment throughout the night while the entire building remained surrounded by uniformed police. One by one they took the people from the apartment. Fortunately, Albina and Paullina were in the country on vacation the night of the arrest.

"My arrest was carried out in the best tradition of arrests. It was done as it is in old movies. Even then I could appreciate it aesthetically, it was done with such pomp. Usually they arrest people without fuss, early in the morning or late at night. But maybe they knew we would be together for only a few hours and they wanted us all."

All twelve were arrested. Six were released after several days, three were sent to psychiatric hospitals, and three stood trial.

During the five months Yuri waited for trial, he was held incommunicado. For two months he refused to say a word to his interrogators. He was placed in solitary confinement.

"Intellectually I was prepared for my arrest. But I wasn't psychologically. The KGB had watched my character very closely, and maybe they knew me better than I knew myself. Solitary confinement was very, very difficult for me. For some people it isn't so hard. They can live longer without talking. But I'm a gregarious person and love talking."

Occasionally Yuri was taken from solitary and placed in a cell with another person.

"When you haven't seen another human being for a period of time you can't imagine how glad you are just to be with someone. It doesn't matter how intellectual or knowledgeable he is or what his political beliefs are. You have to talk to another human being. It was very important, especially for me."

Only in retrospect did Yuri realize that in all likelihood his cellmates were KGB agents. Yuri told one of his cellmates that he was a political prisoner.

"He told me that I was a real hero and once before he met someone like me. He said he spent several months in a cell with him and like me he didn't confess to anything, didn't say a word. My cellmate had only praise for him. But, he told me, they sent him to a psychiatric hospital. He then told me that he met him by chance three months ago in another prison. He said he looked like an old man, his head and hands trembling all the time. He couldn't talk and was a madman now."

Yuri could not know if the story were a fabrication or the truth. But it did frighten him considerably. He did not fear physical torture but had a morbid fear of psychiatric detention.

"Unfortunately I had said this aloud one day and my apartment must have been bugged. So every day during my questioning they threatened to send me to a psychiatric hospital."

The police also took advantage of his love for his family. They offered him a photograph of his daughter to hang in his cell. Yuri regrets having taken it, as it weakened his resistance.

A few times when he returned from questioning, his cellmate would tell him about a woman prisoner he just saw in the corridor. He went on to describe a woman who Yuri came to believe was his wife. Much later Yuri learned from his wife that she had never been arrested.

During the first two months of confinement Yuri did not have a newspaper. The first one they gave him was the August 22 issue of *Pravda,* the entire paper devoted to the story of the Soviet invasion of Czechoslovakia.

"I thought during those long days and nights, if they could do that to a whole country, what could they do with one little, defenseless person."

The various ploys had their effect upon Yuri. One day he began to answer questions. He did not reveal anything about his Moscow friends in the human rights movement, but he did confess to disseminating *samizdat.*

Under an article of Soviet law entitled Anti-Soviet Agitation and Propaganda with the Aim of Undermining the Soviet System, Yuri was found guilty of having distributed fifteen unauthorized books. In addition, he was found guilty of having written protest letters and of planning a demonstration against the Soviet invasion of Czechoslovakia.

"For the authorities this was a great victory. I hadn't been broken completely but I did confess and, let's say, I pleaded guilty. This was a triumph for them. For me it was a great moral disaster. I knew that I was not guilty of breaking any civilized law."

Yuri was sentenced to three years at Modrovia labor camp, section # 11, an area established for political prisoners. While most of the people designated as political prisoners were those convicted of collaboration with the Germans during World War II, nearly a quarter of the prisoners were, like Yuri, prisoners of conscience.

Yuri was put to work making frames for large clocks. This meant cutting lumber, sawing planks, and other types of manual labor for which he had no experience. Yuri became ill with stomach trouble.

"From the first day in the labor camp you have problems with your stomach. They know what they're doing. You are ill all the time with a bad stomach. They give you enough food so you are not starving, but you feel hungry all the time, although not to the point of desperation. You never feel satisfied; you always feel sick. It is very humiliating."

Because of his poor diet, Yuri lost some teeth.

Yuri's reading material was restricted, and he received very few parcels. But one arrived near the end of his sentence and lifted his spirits immeasurably. It came from Freiburg, Germany, and had been sent by an Amnesty International chapter there which had adopted his case two years earlier. It was the first time that he knew that someone outside of Russia cared about him.

"You can't imagine what a feeling a prisoner has when he knows that some organization in the West is thinking about him. It is very great moral support. I didn't know until later that it was Amnesty International that sent me the package but I knew it was some organization. But I'm sure the administration in the labor camp knew where it came from. And they are more careful not to mistreat you when they know that someone in the West supports you."

Yuri's wife was allowed only one visit a year at the labor camp. His brother made one visit during the three years and then was allowed to stay for only an hour.

At the end of his sentence, Yuri was not permitted to return to Leningrad, but instead was restricted to internal exile in the Russian village Tolmachevo, populated, to a large degree, by former political prisoners. He was still separated from his family. Albina and Paullina could visit only once a month.

Yuri, in small ways, resumed his political activity. He did not write letters or disseminate literature but he read all that he could and discussed political affairs with other former prisoners.

Once more he was called upon to demonstrate his moral

courage. Perhaps as an act of redemption for what he perceived as his spiritual collapse in the face of his interrogators while awaiting trial, Yuri risked the possibility of another prison sentence when a friend asked for a favor. This friend had been collecting documents to record the list of victims under Stalin's rule. His friend was under pressure from the government and he asked Yuri to take them from him. Yuri took the documents, went to the forest, buried them, and told his friend where they could be found.

Changes in the climate of international affairs worked to Yuri's advantage. By 1972, the Soviet Union and the United States had developed détente, and the Soviet Union was interested in downplaying its political trials. The KGB approached Yuri and suggested that he apply for immigration papers. They told him that there would be no obstacle placed in the way of his leaving.

Yuri was not eager to emigrate but sensed that he had no real alternative.

"I could stay in the Soviet Union and maybe face another prison sentence. Perhaps I would be placed in a psychiatric hospital or experience another kind of repression. I chose to leave."

The major legal problem seemed to be the fact that Yuri was an ethnic Russian; rarely is a Russian given an exit visa. But since his father was a German Jew who entered Russia at the turn of the century, he was given an Israeli visa despite the fact that his mother was Russian and he considered himself an Orthodox Russian Christian. The authorities also gave an exit visa to Albina and Paullina.

In November 1973, the Handlers entered the United States.

"Those years in Russia were the best days, the best years of my life. Even though I knew what might happen to me I did it anyway. It was my life. All my life I read, all my life I discussed books. Reading is natural for adults. So I had to give out books to my friends even though they were dangerous books. If now I had a choice of beginning everything over again I would do it the same way. I believe in independent thought."

Each August 1, the anniversary of the day of his arrest, Yuri holds a celebration to salute life.

Sister Janice McLaughlin

Rhodesia/Zimbabwe

No one shall be subjected to arbitrary interference with his privacy, family, home or correspondence, nor to attacks upon his honour and reputation. Everyone has the right to the protection of the law against such interference or attacks.

Article 12, Universal Declaration of Human Rights

Zimbabwe, until recently known by most of the world as Rhodesia, was a white settler area, a part of the British Empire. While more than 95 percent of the population is African, nearly half the land had been reserved for white occupancy.

In June 1965 Rhodesia declared itself independent of British rule. No country recognized Rhodesia as an independent state and the United Nations imposed economic sanctions against it.

When Sister Janice McLaughlin was arrested in 1977, Rhodesia, under Prime Minister Ian Smith, was attempting to negotiate an arrangement allowing greater African participation in legislative bodies.

THE PRISON authorities took Sister Janice from her cell in Chikurubi prison and drove her to the Salisbury court. There she met her lawyer.

The lawyer representing the Catholic Commission for Justice and Peace explained the situation to her. He told her that it was not a real trial that she faced, but a publicity stunt on the part of the government. Since her detention two weeks before, her case had received much publicity and had come to the attention of the international press. The government needed to justify its action and was prepared to accuse her of being a Communist.

She told the lawyer that while she was not a Communist she did believe in the kind of socialism she saw in Tanzania. Furthermore, she supported the liberation movement, several groups that the white-ruled government preferred to call terrorists.

The lawyer advised her against stating her political views in the courtroom and recommended that she merely repeat that she had not committed any crime.

Sister Janice entered a packed courtroom. Concern over her detention had reached worldwide proportions.

When Sister Janice took the stand, she ignored her lawyer's advice. Instead, she used the questioning as an opportunity to make explicit her criticism of the present government, stating that Rhodesia needed a total revision in which all people, regardless of color, would share the country's resources equally.

She refused to identify the guerrillas as terrorists, maintaining that they represented an authentic liberation movement and so deserved her support as a religious. When the prosecutor contended that the support of armed struggle was contrary to Christian teaching, Sister Janice responded by referring to the theory of the just war developed by St. Thomas Aquinas, a position widely accepted within the Church that maintains that war is in accord with Christian principles if it is a war on behalf of justice.

The judge adjourned the case, refused her bail, and returned her to Chikurubi prison. She had not expected anything different. She was well aware of the warning issued before Parliament by Minister of Defence Van der Byl: "Where the civilian population involves itself with terrorism, then somebody is bound to get hurt, and one can have little sympathy for those who are mixed up with terrorists when finally they receive the wrath of the security forces."

Sister Janice expected no sympathy nor did she seek it. Instead, this was an opportunity to suffer with the freedom fighters, to be part of the struggle that she had supported since her arrival in

Rhodesia. Her experience was close to elation when, while riding back to prison in the police van, a black prisoner said to her that the Africans who heard her clapped when she refused to call the guerrillas terrorists.

Sister Janice long identified with the underprivileged. As a child in Pittsburgh, she often heard her father rail against the Carnegies and Mellons. But her real awakening came in the 1960s. After her cloistered training and theological studies with Maryknoll, she worked in nearby Ossining. There, for the first time, she saw poverty and discrimination first-hand. By the late 1960s she was involved with anti-war demonstrations, helping to initiate black studies programs and working in community action programs.

She knew that she did not want to be a teaching sister. In 1969 she arrived in Tanzania for study and further training. The next year she moved to Kenya to become press secretary for the Catholic Bishops Conference. The contrast between socialist Tanzania and capitalist Kenya struck Sister Janice and heightened her political sensibilities.

"I became conscious of the fact that I came from an imperialist power. I was aware of being part of the missionary church and that this kind of religious and cultural imperialism existed in many parts of Africa. I was aware of the church structure being near the top, but I saw myself as someone who was in it trying to change it."

As press secretary, Sister Janice met many black revolutionary leaders as they passed through Nairobi. Her sympathies went easily to those who were attempting to wrest power from white-minority governments.

In 1977, Sister Janice applied for the position of press secretary at the Catholic Commission for Justice and Peace in Rhodesia. She wanted to see for herself, from the inside, the process of liberation.

Bishop Donal Lamont interviewed Sister Janice. At that time he was under house arrest after having been convicted of failing to report the presence of guerrillas. Bishop Lamont had taken a position of conscience, knowing full well the government's warning: "Any person giving help to, or failing to report the presence of, these terrorists will be severely punished."

The Commission was constantly running such risks. One aspect of the Commission's work consisted of providing legal assistance to political prisoners and aiding their families. The Commission also published studies of farm workers, domestics, migrants, and other workers. Two of the Commission's booklets were banned by the government soon after their publication.

"I felt proud to be part of a church that was willing to take such risks to be true to its teachings of equality, justice, and freedom. Generally, the church was either on the side of the oppressing colonial powers or it was silent. I was happy to see that in Zimbabwe the church was on the side of the people."

Bishop Lamont defended his actions on theological grounds. He received a ten-year sentence and was finally deported.

Sister Janice's conscience was challenged immediately upon arrival in Salisbury. She discovered that it was illegal to live in a multi-racial dwelling. Rather than live in a segregated convent, she rented an apartment on her own. However, the lease required that she would not allow people of different races to reside with her. She had difficulty signing the lease but felt that since she did not have a visa, only a visitor's permit, it was best not to be deported before she began her work.

By that summer the Commission decided to increase its publications. At that time an Anglo-American team was in the country attempting to work out an internal settlement.

"We felt that the British and Americans were only receiving information given to them by the Smith regime. We wanted to counter that by issuing background reports of our own. We began to write about torture and civilian death and repressive security legislation."

Finished reports were sent abroad to the Catholic Institute for International Relations, the International Commission of Jurists, and Amnesty International.

The government cracked down.

One African staff member, who was also head of the student union at the university, was put under restriction. His mobility was regulated, and he could talk only to those meeting government approval. The Commission learned from other students that he had been beaten by the police.

In July, the government confiscated copies of *Civil War in Rhodesia,* one of the Commission's banned booklets. The Commission received threatening phone calls and the following month the offices were searched once again.

"It was clear to me what price people paid for their convictions. So when the police came to our offices on August 20, it was one more incident in a series of steps to harass the Commission and prevent us from operating effectively.

"They had a search warrant for my office and apartment. I had stacks of paper on my desk and was writing an article about the church in rural areas. I had leaflets that were distributed by the freedom fighters; they found words from songs sung by the freedom fighters. They found so much they took an entire cabinet."

The search warrant stated that they were looking for papers which were likely to "cause fear, alarm and despondency." Sister Janice knew what this meant, for an article in the June 11 Rhodesia *Herald* reported:

> It is now an offence to "communicate to any other person any rumour or report which is likely to cause alarm or despondency." This is punishable by a fine of $100 or three months in jail. Anyone writing, publishing or distributing anything likely to cause alarm or despondency or to lead to action which might be detrimental to national defence, public safety, public order or the termination of the state of public emergency is punishable by a fine of $600 or six months in jail.

The police drove Sister Janice to her apartment, where they continued their search. After finding a book on multinational corporations and a notebook she had kept while in Tanzania, they were ready to leave. Then they saw another notebook, her private diary, one that she began keeping soon after arriving in Africa. The notes in the front of the diary related to church-sponsored discussion groups studying Marxist philosophy of which she had been a part in Kenya.

The police took the books and Sister Janice returned to her office. There she learned that the police had also confiscated material of Father Scholz, another Commission member.

Later that afternoon the police returned again and told Sister

Janice she was wanted for questioning at police headquarters, and she was taken away.

She never reached police headquarters. Instead they took her to her apartment. One officer held her diary while others searched her apartment more thoroughly. They began to read to her from her diary, in particular her comments about Marxism. Although she had decided she would not answer any questions until she could talk to a lawyer, she could not restrain herself in explaining that her notes were made in Kenya and had nothing to do with the situation in Rhodesia. She told them that she did not consider herself a Marxist but a liberal. She then refused to say anything more.

The police warned her that the longer she remained silent the longer would be her detention. After she gathered a toothbrush, toothpaste, and pajamas, they took her to Chikurubi prison.

Three European women with a staff of about thirty African women ran the prison, which, like Rhodesian society, was segregated into African, Coloured, and European sections. The Africans slept forty to a room on mats. They had no hot water and were fed a diet of cornmeal and vegetables. They had no bread or sugar and spent the day—from 6:00 A.M. to 4:00 P.M.—at hard labor.

Sister Janice had a single room with a bed. She had both a bath and shower with hot and cold running water and meals that included meat, vegetables, sugar, tea, bread, and fruit. During the first few days of her detention, she was kept in isolation. However, her African guards seemed concerned about her welfare and took her outside with them to sit on folding chairs in the sun.

She was allowed a brief visit by Commission lawyers who told her that she could be held for thirty days without charges being pressed. They said that the police believed that she was connected with the bombing of Woolworth's in Salisbury, which had taken place about three weeks prior to her detention. In her diary she had made some comments about the bombing. The lawyers advised her not to talk or answer any questions regarding the charges.

The police put pressure on her to discuss the matter. They told her they were prepared to give her safe passage from Rhodesia if she would cooperate with them. She refused the offer.

She was kept in isolation for two weeks. The only person allowed to visit her was the prison chaplain.

"The Bible took on new meaning in my prison cell. The Psalmists, calling from the depths of God's help, seemed to be speaking for all political prisoners, and God's assurances of victory for his oppressed people seemed to predict the downfall of the Smith regime and the creation of an independent Zimbabwe. The story of the conflict between Jesus and those in power seemed to dominate the Gospels. One could easily imagine what he would say about the white racist Rhodesian society. I started to count how many times the Old Testament spoke of God's love for the poor and oppressed, but the number grew so large I lost track. In Chikurubi, religion became relevant. 'God is on our side,' prisoners would say. And I agreed with them."

In the mornings she made her bed, swept and washed the floor of her room, and watered the grass in the courtyard. She was allowed reading material and read a book a day. She requested work and was given a sewing machine and made two new uniforms for herself. She was put in charge of kitchen inventory.

"I was showered with kindness. The Europeans who cooked my food were concerned that I have enough to eat; the Coloured women offered to wash my uniform. Others would let me know whenever one of my visitors had been turned away. The Africans gave me encouragement and support. They were suffering, yet went out of their way to encourage me, knowing they would be punished if they were caught talking to me."

Suddenly Sister Janice was taken to court. It was there that she publicly stated her support for the liberation movement. She was returned to Chikurubi the same day.

Deception was common in prison. She was told that she could write letters to her parents but they were never mailed. The Commission was told that she could receive mail but it was never delivered.

Sister Janice knew that her treatment was mild compared to the Africans'. They began to tell her about their experiences.

"One woman told me that she thought her son was ashamed of her because he never came to see her in prison. She learned only later that he called at the prison each week but was refused entrance. I saw one woman, who was brought to Chikurubi for not paying a bill, wait three days for the prison officials to call her lawyer. 'We're too busy,' was their excuse, and she was still waiting when I left."

Sister Janice watched the kind of quiet resistance this built. One day African prisoners refused to take their noon meal. They objected to the way in which the food had been prepared. One white guard had burnt her sanitary napkin in the fire over which the food was prepared. The Africans thought this was disgusting, so 260 women marched in silence past the food tables and sat mutely on the grass during lunch period.

Sister Janice also learned why some of the other women were imprisoned. She met Angela, who was nineteen years-old. Angela had already spent two years in Chikurubi. She was sentenced to seven years for attempting to cross the border to join the liberation army. The government called her a "terrorist recruit."

Vicky was captured near the Mozambique border. Three of her companions were shot and killed. She was beaten by the military, then sentenced to five years in prison.

Anne was a postulant in a Catholic community of nuns. She and three other religious were arrested while crossing the border.

Margaret was an executive member of a nationalist party. She was seized at Salisbury airport on her return from an overseas conference and detained indefinitely without trial.

Sister Janice knew what accounted for her light treatment.

"I am white, a nun, and an American. If I had been an African I probably would have been tortured. I could have been detained indefinitely or even killed and not a word would have gotten out."

A week after her first court appearance Sister Janice found herself in court again. The judge read from her diary and declared that she was a grave security threat. He announced that formal charges were being prepared against her. It was unclear exactly what this meant but it did mean that the government was prepared to move against her.

She received a hint of what it might be while she was listening to the radio with her guard. A news report said that the government expected that she would be given a minimum sentence of seven years. Her guard was visibly upset by the news and tried to reassure Sister Janice that she would not be in prison that long. The guard implied that the freedom fighters would liberate the prison long before that. The warden, too, tried to soften the news. She told Sister Janice that once formal charges were filed she would be able to see her lawyer and perhaps be released on bail.

When the lawyer did arrive, it was not with bail. Instead, he told her that the government was getting ready to deport her. Sister Janice told him that she did not want to be deported but wanted to stand trial with other Commission members who had also been arrested. The lawyer told her that the others would be better off if her case could be separated from theirs since her charges were so serious.

"I wanted to stay even if it meant remaining in prison. I wasn't worried about receiving a long sentence. Everyone in prison felt that the freedom fighters were going to win in the near future. So many people were in prison for years, and I figured I was part of that.

"If you get involved, you also get involved in persecution. I felt that if the African women could survive and maintain their course, I too could resist and be happy staying with them."

But she never had the chance to demonstrate her solidarity. By 10 o'clock the next morning she was taken to the warden's office to sign for her release. She returned to her apartment, to the Commission office, and to the bank to exchange her Rhodesian dollars for American travelers checks. That afternoon she was put on a plane bound for New York.

The government brought a series of charges against the Commission. In February 1978, the Commission members were finally charged with publishing subversive materials. The case went to court in May and the charges were dropped. The government stated that although the charges were valid, the new internal settlement made it unwise to pursue the case.

In June of that year a Commission member was deported to England. Another member retired to Canada. In July a Commission member, who continued to reside in Salisbury, visited Sister Janice in the United States. While he was in America a hand grenade was thrown into his house in Salisbury.

Meas Sombath

Cambodia/Kampuchea

1. Everyone has the right to freedom of movement and residence within the borders of each state.

2. Everyone has the right to leave any country, including his own, and to return to his country.

Article 13, Universal Declaration of Human Rights

President Richard Nixon said on April 30, 1970: "This is not an invasion of Cambodia. . . . We take this action not for the purposes of expanding the war into Cambodia but for the purposes of ending the war in Vietnam, and winning the just peace we all desire."

In fact, the war in Indochina had crossed into Cambodia more than a year before, when America began secretly bombing that country. Within a few short years, nearly half of all Cambodians left the countryside to seek refuge in the cities. In less than five years, Phnom Penh, the capital, grew from 500,000 to more than three million people.

Cambodia's economy was devastated by the war. Once a rice exporting country, Cambodia became dependent upon American rice supplies as 80 percent of the country's rice paddies were aban-

*doned. Airlifts of food could not keep pace with the growing
number of refugees.*

*When American bombing raids ceased in August 1973, the
number of killed or wounded totalled about 600,000. By then the
Khmer Rouge, the revolutionary army, had increased their hold
on the country. No longer supported by American arms, the Lon
Nol government fell to the Khmer Rouge in April 1975.*

M EAS SOMBATH had not considered leaving Cambodia before,
even though he knew that his work with America's CARE
might be a serious liability when the Khmer Rouge finally seized
control of the country.

On the morning of April 12, 1975, Meas was told of a secret
plan to evacuate all American personnel. Since he worked for a
quasi-official agency, Meas was told that the American Embassy
would provide a place for him on an evacuation helicopter due to
leave within an hour.

"I thought about what he said. Most of the Americans had
already left; that is how I was in charge of much of the emergency
food program. I wasn't sure about going. I wouldn't leave
without first talking to my mother. I wanted to ask her permission. She was the head of the family since my father died.

"There didn't seem to be a special rush. I left the office and
went to a meeting I had scheduled to arrange an airlift of rice to an
area surrounded by the Khmer Rouge. There I had second
thoughts about staying. I thought it would be wisest to leave Cambodia before the new government took over. When things settled
down, I could return and be with my family.

"I left the meeting and went straight to the American Embassy.
Too late. The Embassy was empty. The last helicopter left a half
hour before I arrived. Still I wasn't terribly upset."

For the next several days, Meas ran the food program as best he
could, nearly single-handedly.

Five days later his work came to an abrupt halt. Before day-
break the Khmer Rouge entered Phnom Penh, although throughout the city there remained small areas of active resistance.

From his office window Meas could see black-clad revolutionary soldiers and hear rifle shots. In such confusion, fiction could
not be separated from fact, rumor from truth. Meas did not know

if the stories he heard in the office of mayhem and slaughter were accurate or if they were flashes of paranoia. What he did know was that the Khmer Rouge ideology held intellectuals in disdain. His clothes, his thin, smooth hands, his vocabulary and eyeglasses were marks of the Cambodian elite, clearly one of the enemies of the new government. But what the Khmer Rouge intended to do with the elite class was totally unknown and at that moment unknowable.

Meas heard that the Hotel Phnom, long a center for expatriate activity, had been converted to a safe area under the auspices of the International Committee of the Red Cross. By the time Meas arrived, the hotel was swarming with hundreds of expatriates and Cambodians who feared the revolutionary army. Before midday the grounds were overflowing with the wounded and those seeking a neutral ground.

"I met a friend at the hotel who was a doctor. Since many of the nurses didn't speak Cambodian, he asked if I could be an interpreter. Even as I worked with the medical people inside the rooms converted to surgical theaters, I could hear rifle shots and artillery shells going off."

Later that afternoon, the Khmer Rouge gained control of the area around the hotel compound.

"With megaphones they announced that everyone had to leave the hotel. More than that, they said everyone had to leave the city. They said they wouldn't be responsible for our lives if we stayed."

That was the first hint at what was to become a major element of the new government's policy: the reduction of urban areas to small towns.

"We put together stretchers, then went straight for the French Embassy where we sought asylum. The Europeans were taken right in but they turned Cambodians away."

The French claimed they could not handle everyone. Fearing for their lives, many Cambodians rushed the fence surrounding the French grounds, only to be repulsed by the guards. Denied admission at the gate, Meas decided to return home.

"I think being turned away by the French saved my life. A few days later the Khmer Rough went to the Embassy to demand that all Cambodians leave. The few who were there were taken away and executed."

Meas told his family what had happened, what he had seen. Meas's mother expressed her unhappiness that he had not left with the Americans days earlier. She predicted that there was nothing good in their future.

The orders from the Khmer Rouge were clear and unequivocal. Phnom Penh was to be evacuated. More than three million residents, refugees, and squatters had to leave. The Khmer Rouge wanted everyone out in the countryside growing rice.

The Sombath family—Meas's mother, his brother, his brother's wife and children, a sister, plus three orphaned children of another sister—faced an immediate problem. They had no relatives in the countryside to whom they could turn. Meas had been born in Phnom Penh. His father had left his native village many years before. Yet they could not stay in the only home that Meas had ever known.

Meas took off his glasses—the sign of being an intellectual—and left them behind, as the family piled whatever belongings they could into and on top of their three cars. At first Meas could barely see without his glasses. In time he would adjust.

The small caravan took a highway west out of the city. They quickly became absorbed in the mass of people—people on foot, in cars, in carts, with animals, carrying their belongings in whatever way they could—a mass migration, an exodus of massive proportions. It was a move to change the face of Cambodia.

Radio Phnom Penh: "More than two thousand years of Cambodian history has virtually ended."

That night they slept beside their cars.

The next day they continued their journey without a destination. Soldiers, lined along the roads to expedite movement, explained that the city needed to be evacuated because they anticipated an American aerial attack. Hanoi had been bombed in 1972, so such an attack seemed feasible.

The exodus had slowed to a near standstill. The roads were jammed with cars, people walking, people fainting or growing ill, taken to one side to be ministered to by the family or left to die, children walking, infants carried, old people helped, people injured in the last days of battle, patients taken from hospital beds moving en masse.

Two of their cars were commandeered by the Khmer Rouge. On

the third day they had no more gas. They took turns pushing the car. Each night they stopped in place, prepared a small quantity of rice and slept on the road.

In nine days they had traveled less than ten miles.

"The Khmer Rouge told us to go to our native village. We told the soldier we were all born in Phnom Penh. He asked about our father's village. We couldn't remember the name of the village right away. But then my mother remembered where he had been born. The soldier ordered us to go there."

Tonle Bati was nearby.

"When we got to the village, the Khmer Rouge recorded all our belongings—our car, whatever rice remained, our two radios, even our clothes. We thought that soon we would be allowed to return to the city. We didn't know then that we were supposed to stay in Tonle Bati forever."

The village had been under Khmer Rouge control since 1970. When the Sombaths and other refugees arrived, the village was prepared to absorb them into communal living. Under the supervision of families who were longtime supporters of the Khmer Rouge, each of the arrivals would learn a new way of life. Meas, his mother, and three nieces were assigned to one family, his brother and his family to another, and his sister and her children to a third.

On the first day at Tonle Bati the family dyed their clothes black, to conform to revolutionary attire.

Radio Phnom Penh: "Democratic Kampuchea is one huge worksite; wherever one may be, something is being built. The people, children, men and women, and the old people of all cooperatives are enthusiastically building mini-dikes."

Two days after their arrival at Tonle Bati, Meas and his brother began work on a dam five miles from the village. More than five thousand people worked there.

"When we first arrived we were given some tools and told what to do. We were told only once. We couldn't ask questions. We didn't dare. The soldiers gave us our instructions and we knew we had to follow them. They didn't stand guard over us all the time; it wasn't like a prison. But we all understood very well what would happen to us if we didn't do what we were told."

Radio Phnom Penh: "The soldiers set an example at worksites

—to protect the revolution and the country they keep their vigilance razor-sharp, as though they were sharpening a knife."

For the first two days, Meas and his brother walked to the site each morning from Tonle Bati. They were then ordered to remain at the barracks at the dam site.

Meas was encouraged by the presence of his brother. His consolation came from knowing that his family's condition was not unique. He knew that everyone in Kampuchea was at work under arduous conditions, often during night hours, without adequate food. Respite from labor came during political education programs. The daily regimen of lectures stressed leaving the past behind and learning better the virtue of courage to fight to preserve the revolution.

"We were told that if we couldn't follow the pace of the revolution, we would be separated from the others."

Several weeks after being assigned to the dam project, Meas's brother was told that he was wanted in another village for a celebration. First he could return to Tonle Bati. Not wanting to remain alone, Meas requested permission to go with him.

In Tonle Bati the family discussed the invitation. Perhaps there was a ceremony of some sort that, for propaganda purposes, needed a large crowd present. But the family reached the conclusion that that was not it at all. Since the Khmer Rouge had a reputation for austerity and generally discouraging festivities of any sort, something else lay behind the invitation. They suspected that the Khmer Rouge knew that he had been a police officer in Phnom Penh and had therefore been designated as an enemy of the people. The invitation was not for a festival but for his own execution.

Meas proposed that he and his brother attempt an escape to Thailand. If they stayed, they would surely be killed. The mother concurred. She believed that the women and children would be safe but that the men were in serious trouble. She gave her blessing.

Meas's brother was not convinced. He argued that the border was a long way, and there were many soldiers and cadres. They could never make it safely. It might be better to go to the celebration. Then, if it were in fact a death trip, he could attempt an escape.

While the family tried to persuade the brother to leave, Meas went to the village head, told him he wanted a pass for himself and his brother to look for part of their family which had been separated during the migration from Phnom Penh.

"The village head didn't know that my brother had received an invitation at the worksite. If he did, I don't think he would have issued us the passes."

The two three-day passes stated that they were looking for their families. However, his brother had reached a firm decision not to leave. A sense of family loyalty, more than a fear of encountering Khmer Rouge or hope that the celebration would be benign, prevented him from leaving his mother, wife, children, and sister.

Meas too felt the strong family ties. But he could not agree with his brother. His mother understood too. Whether they liked it or not, a new society was being built and the old ways had to change.

Radio Phnom Penh: "Every day goes by in a holiday atmosphere."

Using a communal bicycle, Meas headed west, his pass in his pocket. At the end of three days, Meas forged a new pass.

"I lied to soldiers whenever they stopped me. I told them I was on my way back from a construction site and was headed to my village. At one point, I had to hide for two days because the Khmer Rouge were stopping everyone who moved along the road. I didn't think I could get away with my story under intense scrutiny."

Meas found an abandoned house. He stayed there until a farmer warned Meas that the Khmer Rouge suspected that someone was in the house who did not belong to the village.

By then the roadchecks had lightened. But as a precaution, Meas stayed on the backroads as he pedaled west to the border.

After nearly three weeks of circumspection, caution, and deceit, Meas decided to take a risk. He encountered a convoy headed towards Sisophon, a small city near the Thai border. He asked the convoy chief for a lift.

"He asked me if I had a pass. I said I did. He wanted to know if it had the seal of the provincial committee. It didn't have any seal at all, but I told him it did. Luckily the bluff worked. He didn't ask to see it.

"Then he wanted to know if I could drive a truck. I'd never

driven a truck in my life but I told him I was an experienced truck driver. I had to hide my educated background. So I pretended to be a person who worked with his hands. If I couldn't be a peasant, at least I could be a driver."

The work chief told him to put his bicycle in the back of one of the trucks. He told him to find a truck with no driver which was chained to one in front, get in, and steer.

In that way, Meas became a truck driver, as part of a convoy of disabled vehicles being gathered from the countryside.

Meas had traveled four hundred miles from Tonle Bati. But he knew that the last few miles would be the most difficult to negotiate. Sisophon occupied a strategic point near the Thai border and would be heavily patroled.

When they reached Sisophon, Meas explained to the convoy head that his family had been evacuated from the area. But since he was a mechanic and a driver, he wanted to work with his unit. The unit chief agreed.

Meas knew less about mechanics than he did about driving a truck. Without his glasses, he had a difficult time seeing the small pieces.

"I learned very quickly. I put everything, all my concentration into the engines."

Within days he became expert. He had summoned out of the deepest part of his being the ability to compensate for his poor eyesight and his untrained hands.

Each night he called upon Buddha for protection, for his survival and the safety of his family.

Radio Phnom Penh: "In the past, in the days of Lon Nol—the archtraitor, the overcorrupted, the highly harmful, the stooges of America—you were poor and oppressed. You could never enjoy life because you suffered from poverty and hunger. Now, under the enlightened and intelligent leadership of the revolutionary organization, you live in happiness and prosperity."

"I never saw an execution. But I did see twenty to thirty people tied together; then they disappeared. I often found fields full of bodies and skeletons. People I worked with just disappeared during the night. One of the drivers had a slight accident with his truck. A few soldiers in the back were injured. They brought him to the security office. I never saw him again."

Later that year Meas went with his unit to Banteay Chmar, about twenty-five miles from Thailand. When they arrived, Meas asked his unit chief if he could take some time to look for his family. Since this was the ostensible reason for his being in Sisophon, the chief agreed.

Meas walked toward the border, intending to reach jungle cover before dark. The sun set before he made it, and, remembering the assistance received from a farmer once before, he asked for shelter. The farmer invited Meas to sleep on the verandah and brought him some food.

The next morning Meas was awakened by five men; the farmer was pointing him out. He was taken to the village chief who requested to see his pass. Meas explained that he did not have one, that he was a driver from Sisophon who was looking for his family. The village head had Meas's bag searched. In it were found some rice and clothing.

He was immediately bound. The village head knew that he would be carrying food and clothes only if he were planning to escape. The commune committee was summoned to deal with the situation.

The committee notified the unit chief from Meas's brigade, who quickly arrived to decide the fate of his worker.

The commune wanted to hold Meas for another night, perhaps to execute him the following morning. The unit chief argued that he was already short of drivers and would be unable to bring back all the vehicles to Sisophon without Meas.

The commune released Meas.

The Constitution of Democratic Kampuchea: "Actions violating the law of the people's State are as follows: Hostile and destructive activities that threaten the popular State shall be subject to the severest form of punishment.

"Other cases shall be handled by means of constructive re-education in the framework of the State of people's organizations."

Meas found himself under extreme pressure for nearly a year. In addition to his usual work he was conscripted for ditch digging in the fields around Sisophon. He helped plant rice, husk, and harvest. Because so many animals had either been killed during the war or starved afterwards, Meas was used to pull ox carts when no draft animals were available.

He felt as if he were constantly being watched, with the authorities waiting for him to make the slightest mistake. He knew that there was no margin for error.

Yet, he was never distracted from his goal: escape. He thought about it, planned for it, and prayed for it. He waited for an opportunity.

It came when his unit was ordered to pick up timber in a wooded area less than twenty-five miles from the Thai border. Between the road and the border was a section filled with land mines and booby traps, devices that had been used with great success during the war. The area, a dense jungle, designated as a no man's land, was heavily patroled.

"I made several trips into this area and each time I studied the location. I concluded that the shortest distance to Thailand was somewhere between the timber pick-up point and the town where I had been held by the commune. I thought there was nothing between the road and the border except jungle."

The crew stopped to gather the timber. When they were finished, the driver, a soldier, and a mechanic sat in the cab. Meas volunteered to sit in the back, riding on the lumber. The truck began to move down the road.

Meas was ready. When they reached the point closest to Thailand, he leaped from the back. But one of the branches caught his shirt and instead of being thrown from the truck he was dragged behind it in the dirt road, his skin being torn. He could not call for help.

Fortunately, before he lost consciousness, the truck hit a pothole, jarred the timber, and shook Meas loose. He scrambled to his feet and ran into the thick foliage. The truck continued; no one knew he was gone.

Meas had learned enough about the jungle border to know to keep off the paths, the most likely place to be mined. He moved cautiously but persistently through the jungle, unconcerned with the injuries he had received while being dragged. He did not know where he was but he knew that if he kept going west he would eventually reach Thailand.

He had only a canteen of water. He finished it the second day. He would not eat or drink from then on. He feared being poisoned.

He managed to avoid landmines but was caught in a trap that

had been covered with leaves. He landed upon sharp, wooden spikes.

"I thought I died then. I don't know what I did but somehow I managed to use all my remaining strength and pull myself out. Then I continued to run, I was so scared. I prayed all the time."

Meas managed his way across the border but not to freedom. When Thai soldiers discovered him, they handcuffed him, charged him with illegal entry, and placed him in a local jail. They charged him with crossing the border without proper documents.

For the first time, Meas was imprisoned. But he had used his wits to leave Kampuchea and he would do it again, this time without deception or bravado. He simply requested that he be granted permission to write a letter. This he addressed to a friend of his from the CARE office who had been transferred to Bangkok. With this friend's help, Meas was transferred from the country jail to a refugee camp. There he wrote another letter, this time to the American Embassy in Bangkok. Since no one knew exactly what to do with his letter, it was passed from department to department until someone recognized his name and interceded on his behalf.

This friend then organized a campaign for Meas. Many Americans in the Bangkok office wrote to their representatives in Washington, asking them to petition the State Department. Several months later, Meas was released from the camp with authorization to enter the United States.

Meas does not know what happened to his family. Their names do not appear on any refugee list. He has no way of reaching them. And once more his country became a battlefield, as the Vietnamese moved to replace the Khmer Rouge government.

"I don't want to even think about those times. Any tragedy, any difficulty is sad. But I want to make people understand, to make them know that they can't take anything for granted. People suffer. As human beings we can't let such tragedies happen again. That's why I tell my story."

Martin Sostre

United States

All are equal before the law and are entitled without any discrimination to equal protection under the law.

Article 7, Universal Declaration
of Human Rights

Civil rights activities intensified in the early 1960s. Sit-ins protesting legal discrimination occurred throughout the South. Protests against economic and housing inequities took place in the North. However, 1963 marked the beginning of a pattern of violence that was to persist for several years. Mississippi leader Medgar Evers was murdered, and four school children died in a church explosion in Birmingham.

Race riots broke out in several cities that year. In 1964, racial violence continued in Jacksonville, where, for the first time, Molotov cocktails were used. Police were used to quell racial disturbances in many cities that summer, and the National Guard was used in Rochester.

In 1965, thirty-four were killed in the Watts riots. By 1966, racial violence had appeared to become part of the American scene. Some newspapers began keeping tally sheets. The pattern continued through 1967 and 1968.

At the same time, the United States experienced the upsurge of student anti-war protests. Street demonstrations had become a way of life, although one that many American's felt they could not tolerate.

It was in the midst of the growing fear that America's stability was disintegrating that Martin Sostre was arrested in New York.

IN 1979, when former U.N. Ambassador Andrew Young outraged many of his fellow Americans by charging that there are hundreds and perhaps thousands of political prisoners in the United States, Martin Sostre found himself in full accord with Young.

"The difference between America and the other countries is money," Martin said. "In America, they can spend $100,000 or more on court expenses just to imprison one political dissident. If you were in Argentina, you would just disappear. You'd be walking down the street and a carload of goons would grab you, put a blanket on your head, take you to a basement, and someone would get your nuts or your hand or your toes in a vise and keep it up until you signed a confession saying what they wanted you to say.

"But here they can afford to make everything legal, keep up a semblance of law and justice. They can pick juries, pay off witnesses, tie up the courts for years. They have the money to play around with, so they can say that they don't have any political prisoners. They can frame you up on criminal charges so that way you won't be able to prove that you're a political prisoner."

Martin describes himself as a revolutionary anarchist. In 1968, he received a prison sentence of thirty to forty-one years for allegedly having sold $15 worth of heroin in his Buffalo bookstore. Ramsey Clark, Julian Bond, Jean-Paul Sartre, and Andrei Sakharov, on behalf of Amnesty International, felt Martin had been framed on criminal charges and had not received a fair trial. They also expressed concern about his harsh treatment in prison. Each believed that Martin's imprisonment was attributable to his radical politics. In other words, Martin Sostre was one of America's political prisoners.

Nine years as a political prisoner, much of it spent in solitary confinement, did not dampen the ardor of the bald, black Puerto

Rican. Soon after his release from prison—an act of clemency by New York's Governor Hugh Carey—Martin was on a speaking tour around the country. He knew his parole could be revoked at any time, but he refused to temper his rhetoric and continued to stress his belief that America needed revolutionary change. "I'm not behind bars," he said, "but I'm still a prisoner. My parole doesn't end until 2001. But they couldn't intimidate me in solitary confinement, and they won't be able to intimidate me out here."

By the time Martin was released in 1976, facts regarding his frame-up, the unreliability of the witnesses against him, the time he spent in solitary confinement as punishment for his determination not to be broken spiritually, and the repeated beatings inflicted on him by prison guards were on the public record. Revelations of surreptitious and illegal activities by various police departments and the FBI helped support Martin's contention that he was truly an American prisoner of conscience.

Born in Harlem in 1923, Martin left high school after two years to help his family through the Great Depression. Jobs were scarce in New York, especially for a young, semi-educated black man with a Puerto Rican accent. So Martin learned to hustle the street. Though he was not aware of it at the time, he also learned the rudiments of radicalism.

"My father was a talking communist—he talked about it but never did anything," Martin recalls. "He made speeches at home, always referring to the capitalists in Spanish as 'the vandals.' He belonged to a club in Harlem that was supposedly leftist. But I just remember him playing checkers and dominoes.

"I got my education on the street. I listened to Vito Marcantonio, the radical Congressman from Harlem. I heard Paul Robeson and listened to Ben Davis, of the Communist Party, on street corners."

Martin Sostre did not take politics seriously then. When he returned from the Army in 1946, still unskilled and lacking direction, he returned to the streets. No one was surprised when he was arrested in 1952 and convicted on a drug charge carrying a six-to-twelve-year sentence. Some could argue that he was the victim of a system of inequities, that he was a prisoner because society was unjust and racist, but he was not yet a political prisoner. His conversion to political activism did not occur until after he entered

Attica Prison, and he did not become a political prisoner until he was arrested again fifteen years later.

Attica served as the crucible in which Martin developed his political convictions. Only while in prison did the slogans he heard on the street corners and the radical literature he saw displayed at Michaeux's bookstore on Lenox Avenue begin to make sense. His prison experiences could be understood—and made more tolerable—within the radical framework to which he had been exposed.

Martin's initiation into political activism came through his contact with the Black Muslims: "I identified with Malcolm X because he was a street hustler, like me. And he was very political. There were no other radicals in prison at that time. They were the only group with a formed ideology. I went for the political part of the Muslims. The religious part didn't interest me."

Convinced that the system could be used against itself, Martin began to study law—a risky venture, since prisoners were not allowed access to law books, and prison regulations prohibited prisoners from offering each other legal advice. Nonetheless, an underground network of jailhouse lawyers existed at Attica, and when one left prison Martin inherited his "law library." He read the U.S. Constitution and concluded that Muslims had a right to worship without interference—a right denied them at Attica. He brought suit against the State of New York and won.

Emboldened by his success, Martin began to challenge the prison system on behalf of other prisoners. During a shakedown of his cell, guards found another prisoner's legal documents. For this infraction of prison rules, they lifted Martin's yard and commissary privileges.

Harassment intensified in proportion to Martin's reputation as a jailhouse lawyer. Over the next few years he challenged the all-white composition of the New York Parole Board, enjoined prison authorities from opening and reading prisoners' mail, and brought suit against the prison system of enlisting the aid of prisoners against other prisoners as a condition for parole.

Five years of Martin's twelve-year sentence were spent in the primitive conditions of solitary confinement: "I slept on a concrete floor with no bed and no mattress. All I had was a blanket which they gave me at night and took away early the next morn-

ing. The floor was so hard and cold that I could sleep only ten
minutes in one position. In order to deal with this, I taught myself
yoga. There was no light, no running water, no toilet. You had a
shit bucket that was emptied once a day, about 8 A.M. You would
have to smell it all day long."

Martin served his full sentence, never making parole. His self-
education and fortitude won him the enmity of the entire prison
system. By the time he was released, he had gained a reputation as
a trouble-making radical.

"That experience fully politicized me," he says. "I got a taste of
how brutal and vicious and lawless the system is. Once you're
caught up in their web, you're in trouble."

Three years after his release, trouble caught Martin again. He
had entered prison in the quiet 1950s, but he emerged in the rising
turmoil that came to characterize the 1960s. America was confronted with its racial dilemma in a new and forceful way—sit-
ins, demonstrations, the murder of civil rights workers, urban
riots.

With $400 and donated labor supplied by friends who sup-
ported Martin's radicalism, he opened a bookstore in Buffalo,
stocked with Marxist and black nationalist literature. It was the
sort of bookstore the city had not seen before. As the campus of
the State University became a major center for student dissidents,
the Afro-Asian Bookstore attracted student radicals, both black
and white, in a city proud of its white, ethnic heritage.

In January 1967, a city detective visited Martin at his store and
asked why he was selling "commie literature." The spectre of a
new McCarthyism loomed real for Martin. He remembered his
stay at Sing Sing—and the night the light in his cell dimmed as the
Rosenbergs were executed. But he had confronted authority before, in prison, and he would not let the minor inquisition daunt
him.

"I have a First Amendment right to sell any literature I want,"
he said. "I buy these books from other bookstores and publishers.
So what's wrong with that?"

"You could do better with some other kind of literature," he
was told. "This kind of stuff can get you in trouble."

Several months later, an FBI agent identified himself to Martin, reminded him that he had not been out of prison long, and

implied that the store was a Communist front. Martin invited him to search the store.

"OK, Marty," said the agent. "OK. If that's the way you want it, I'm not going to argue with you."

Martin noticed that his bookstore had come under constant police surveillance. An unmarked car routinely passed the store, slowing as it passed, a detective peering through the glass front. Occasionally, the car was parked at the end of the street so the police could watch people come and go. The detectives made no attempt to conceal their watch, and used it as a form of intimidation.

The urban turmoil that erupted around the country in 1967 reached Buffalo on June 27, when a ten-block area, the neighborhood in which the Afro-Asian Bookstore was located, experienced a night of riots. The city called out seventy-five riot police to restore order. The outrage escalated the following night, with 1,500 protesters in the streets. Before the night was over, fourteen people had been wounded, shot either by the police or by rioters. On the third night, 100 were arrested. The police, pelted with stones and bricks, responded with tear gas and shotguns. By night's end, eighteen were injured, twelve suffering shotgun wounds. The riots climaxed on the fourth night, when seventy-eight were injured and more than 200 arrested. The damage was centered in the ghetto itself, but one of the few stores to remain untouched was the Afro-Asian Bookstore. Amid broken glass, burnt buildings, and rubble, the bookstore stood intact.

Black leaders blamed the riots on the lack of jobs and poor police-community relations. But Mayor Frank Sedita said, "My information is that the trouble has not been started by local people." It was the bogeyman of the "outside troublemaker," and Martin soon found himself identified as one of the "out-of-towners" to whom the mayor had alluded.

The bookstore was located next to a bar, a known hangout for drug addicts and dealers. A few days after the riot, Arto Williams, a man Martin had often seen hanging out at the bar, came into the bookstore to ask a favor. He said that he was going downtown and had some money he did not want to take with him. He said he would be right back. Martin took $15 and put it in his cash register.

The request was not unusual. "People used to leave all sorts of things in the bookstore," Martin recalls. "Once a woman left her two-year-old kid while she went shopping. People left packages for us to watch. Once this guy, Arto Williams, came in and left a suit for me to watch that he had just taken out of the cleaners. He had to go downtown and didn't want to carry it. He used to hang out at the bar all the time. I used to see him standing in front with other junkies. So I didn't think anything of it when he asked me to hold some money."

Arto Williams never returned for the money. Instead, later that evening, when Martin was in the back of the store, he heard a commotion in the front. As he looked up, he saw about a dozen men grab the clerk and push her into a chair. Martin ran to the front and was knocked to the ground.

The intruders handcuffed Martin behind his back, then identified themselves as Buffalo police. They produced a warrant and told him that he was under arrest for the sale of drugs, arson, and inciting a riot. At the police station they added the charge of assaulting police officers.

Arto Williams was one of the main witnesses against Martin. In June of that summer, Williams had been arrested for burglary and, as a multiple offender, faced a possible thirty-year sentence. The police contended that Williams called them from jail, telling them that he knew a drug dealer and would cooperate in exchange for a reduced sentence. It was at that point, the police claimed, that they put Martin under surveillance. They watched the store for more than a month and on the day of the alleged sale of drugs watched from across the street, photographing the exchange. However, the photographs were never developed because the camera had been loaded with the wrong film. But proof of the sale was the $15 in marked bills found in the cash register.

The trial lasted less than half a day, and Martin was sentenced to prison again, this time for thirty to forty-one years, the maximum under law.

All charges except the sale of drugs had been dropped. No mention was made of the bookstore or of Martin's radical politics. The court record would not reveal that the case had been a political trial. Martin was tried as an ordinary criminal within the framework of the judicial system. Unlike political prisoners in other countries, he would have no dossier stamped "Political Prisoner." He was Martin Sostre, twice convicted on drugs.

Martin wasted no time resuming his activism within the prison. While a defense committee was formed on his behalf, he attempted to organize a prisoners' labor union and initiated a new round of suits to protect prisoners' rights. He called it his "campaign for survival."

"I wasn't doing these things for anybody else. I'm not Jesus Christ. I tried to do it for myself. When I took the cases to court, I did it for Martin Sostre. But I knew that Martin Sostre didn't live in a vacuum, and if I won a decision it would affect all prisoners. I wanted more freedom and if I won it for me, everyone would have it."

Martin won cases against Attica's internal punishment system on the grounds that it did not offer inmates due process; he won another case which allowed prisoners to receive mail uncensored.

He was not always successful, and a lost case often led to severe punishment. Defying prison regulations, Martin grew a moustache and beard. When he refused to shave, he was taken to solitary confinement.

Conditions in solitary confinement had improved since Martin had first been confined there in the 1950s. Now he had a mattress, blanket, and sheets, a flush toilet, cold running water, and a sink. There was one light and he was allowed an hour's exercise each day. The only personal property allowed were law books—a new prisoner's right and one upon which Martin insisted. He filled his cell with books.

Because of the various suits he had pending, he did not spend all of his time in solitary. He was allowed out for preparation and presentation. Although every item he had in his cell had to go through prison authorities before reaching him, guards insisted upon rectal searches each time he left and returned to his cell.

Martin refused to submit to the deliberate humiliation. "There's no reason for the search. You don't even have a safety pin in solitary. You have no commissary, no personal items, no nothing. Just the prison clothes they give you. But they make you bend over and they stand back, laughing, saying things like 'Look at that asshole. I'd like to put this stick into it.' I refused to do it and brought suit against the prison system."

Martin won this case, too. The judge ruled that rectal examinations in solitary confinement were dehumanizing and needlessly degrading. Recognizing the harsh treatment dealt out to Martin because of his constant court challenges, the judge ruled that he had been subjected to "cruel and unusual punishment . . . for his ideas," and awarded $13,000 in damages.

In 1973, two separate developments helped Martin's case. First, Sergeant Alvin Gristmacher, the police sergeant in charge of Martin's arrest and one of the state's two key witnesses against him, was dismissed from the Buffalo Police Department. He had been indicted for his part in the disappearance of a significant amount of heroin from the police evidence locker. This not only impugned his character but also raised the possibility that the heroin Williams had turned over to the police had been obtained by Gristmacher from the police locker.

More significant than the Gristmacher matter was the retraction of the testimony of the other witness, Arto Williams. Williams decided to recant while taking part in a drug rehabilitation program in California. During one of the rap sessions in which each person confesses to the weakness of his own character, Williams said the worst thing he had ever done was to frame an innocent man. He said that he had been arrested in Buffalo and faced a long sentence. While in jail, the police offered to release him without bail if he would give marked money to someone. The only thing he knew about this person was that he was a political activist.

With the therapy group's encouragement, Williams wrote a letter to a New York judge—the same judge who had ruled favorably on Martin's case regarding rectal searches. Upon receiving an affidavit from Williams, Martin's lawyer requested a retrial.

Although momentum was building in Martin's favor, he still encountered trouble in prison. On May 19, as he was being taken from his cell in solitary to attend the hearing, the guards ordered him to bend over for a rectal search. Martin cited the court ruling barring such practices, but the guards ignored his protests and insisted. When Martin refused again, the guards grabbed him.

"I struggled the best I could. But I'm not a superman. Eventually they subdued me, threw me to the concrete floor while I was naked. They laid me out spread-eagle, four guards each holding down my arms and legs with both hands, while kneeling on each arm and leg with a knee. They one guard straddled me and hit me right in my kidneys. They didn't hit me in the face because that would show in court. But they gave me about six or seven shots in the kidneys."

Each day, as he was moved from his cell to the court, Martin was beaten. On May 29, he submitted a complaint under the Civil Rights Act, stating, "I have become a victim of systematic repression and brutality for having exercised my right to challenge in Federal Court their violation of prisoners' human and constitutional rights."

In its deliberate and thorough manner, Amnesty International had been investigating Martin's case. It concluded that he was, in fact, a political prisoner who had been falsely accused. That was the turning point. Amnesty was recognized for its impartiality, and when it announced its findings, others rallied to his defense.

Though Arto Williams admitted in court that he had framed Martin, stating that he would have done anything to avoid a return to prison, a motion to hold a new trial on the heroin charge was denied. In October 1975, the U.S. Supreme Court refused on technical grounds to hear the case.

Martin refused to compromise his principles, finding more strength with each round. As he wrote in a letter to the court, "They may succeed in beating me to death, but they shall never succeed in forcing me to relinquish what in the final analysis are the final citadels of my personality, human dignity and self-respect."

It seemed all recourse had been closed to Martin, but moves to free him continued to mount through extra-legal channels. Just as public pressure and politics had put him behind bars in 1967, public pressure would be responsible for his release. Petitions, telephone calls, and letters arrived regularly at the State Capitol in Albany. Stories about Martin and letters from him appeared in newspapers and magazines. His recognition as an American prisoner of conscience was a source of embarrassment to politicians. The tipping point seemed to be a letter to Governor Carey from Andrei Sakharov, the famed Soviet dissident. Writing as a member of Amnesty International's Moscow Group, Sakharov appealed to Carey to intercede on Martin's behalf.

On Christmas Day 1975, Martin finally received clemency. The state did not overturn his conviction or offer amnesty. It simply released him early, never admitting that he was a political prisoner or that the state had been wrong in imprisoning him. The official record remained clean: America has no political prisoners.

Since he was released on parole, Martin is still technically a prisoner. "If I keep out of trouble, keep my nose clean, they may review my parole this year," he says. "It's up to my parole officer and Albany. I'm not living in fear of being locked up again, but I know it might happen. If I were afraid, I would never have done what I've done. I was a dissident in prison and I'm a dissident now. As long as there is oppression, I'll remain a dissident."

Martin's determination to see a better world was strengthened by his prison experiences. "People have to be made aware, things have to be publicized. Oppression, like crime, breeds and operates in darkness and silence. Once the cat is out of the bag, freedom of expression will exist. It will become very difficult to get rid of people. Wherever dissidents get publicity—in Russia, China, Chile, Argentina, America—and the world knows about it, they'll be released, or at least treated humanely. It's only when no one knows about it that state officials can really torture and do whatever they want. The only reason I'm out of prison instead of in is because of pressure and publicity."

Irena Lasota

Poland

**Everyone has the right to freedom of peaceful assembly and asso-
ciation.**

*Article 20, Universal Declaration
of Human Rights*

 *Wladyslaw Gomulka emerged as Poland's leader following
World War II. By 1948 he was forced from power for not adhering
closely enough to Stalin's policies and was imprisoned. By 1956,
two years after his release, he was returned to power as the First
Secretary of the Communist Party.*

 *During the next four years, Poland experienced a period of lib-
eral domestic policies. However, this approach split the Party into
opposing factions: those who believed the liberalization did not
go far enough, and those who believed that it had gone too far. In
order to maintain his control, Gomulka reaffirmed the supreme
position of the Party, actively discouraged dissent and intellectual
criticism, instituted new controls over the Catholic church and
curtailed experiments in worker councils.*

 *When Irena Lasota entered Warsaw University in 1962, that
university was one of the few remaining islands of intellectual
freedom.*

W HEN IRENA LASOTA entered Warsaw University in 1962, the beginning of the worldwide student revolts was still two years away. Irena would help formulate and lead a massive strike against the college administration—and against the government itself—which would lead to the most serious and vocal protest against the Gomulka government since his return to power more than ten years before. Because of her activities, Irena would not graduate, would be imprisoned and eventually exiled.

Much social criticism has originated in universities, with the politically neutral campus serving as a staging area for protest. But in the early 1960s, students began to see the university as part of the establishment. Colleges became the focus of the protests themselves. Thus, campuses no longer provided a haven, a place into which the police would not enter. When students moved to shut down the college, the university administration called upon the police to remove the students.

From country to country, from continent to continent the pattern was the same. In Berkeley, in London, in Rome, students closed classes, shouted slogans, and offered lists of demands. Following the familiar scenario, Irena and her fellow students challenged Warsaw University and the Polish government.

Political dissidence was nothing new in Irena's family. In the 1920s her father, a Polish Jew, moved to Paris where, as a painter, he became part of the avant garde whose manners and art turned bourgeois life upside down. During the Depression, he joined the French Communist Party, and, when Spain became the first battleground of World War II, he fought against the fascists. He remained in France throughout the war, married a French woman, and returned in 1947 to Poland, father of two-year old Irena.

"My father's surname was Hirszowicz, obviously a Jewish name. When he returned to Poland to begin work for the Party, they told him that it would be advisable for him to change his name to a Polish one. Anti-semitism was common in Poland and it would be best for everyone if it weren't so obvious that he was a Jew. So he changed his name to Lasota. This is the name I grew up with."

Until 1950, Irena's father worked in the technical assistance sector of Party intelligence. As part of a purge that year, many who lived abroad during the war years were removed from responsible positions. After a year's unemployment, he found a job with a publishing house.

Irena's interest in politics was developed during her high school years, in particular by her association with the Girl Scouts. There she met Jacek Kuron, a Scout organizer. "He liked to work with people. And although scouting is down at the bottom of important official Polish organizations, he found that he could enter into the official framework by working with the Scouts." While the group performed typical scouting functions such as camping and hiking, there were also discussion groups that concerned themselves with social issues.

Part of Irena's scouting experience included drama workshops, initiated by Kuron. "One of the plays I wrote was about how the teachers hated the children and the children hated the teachers. The teachers decided to go on strike and the students wanted to burn down the school. Finally, the school burns down and everyone hopes that they will be able to build a new one."

The government hoped the Scouts would find something else to do. It was the final play put on by the group; the government disbanded the drama workshop and dismissed Kuron from his position.

However, Irena did not lose contact with her political mentor. When she entered the university, Kuron was on the faculty, continuing to work with young people to develop their social and political awareness.

Irena immediately entered into student politics by joining the officially sanctioned Socialist Youth. She quickly grew impatient with the group. "I didn't like most of the students. They weren't very interesting. They were rigid and simply followed the dictates of the Party. That didn't appeal to me."

What did appeal to Irena was independent, critical, and original thinking. She left the Socialist Youth to become part of a loose network of incipient dissident students who began to formulate a new perspective on Polish society. Inspired by similar groups forming in other communist nations and by the international student movement, the students began to compare actual university policies with the university's stated objectives. For example, when she and a group of fellow students examined the make-up of the student body at the university, they found that while Polish workers and peasants constituted about 70 percent of the country's population, both these groups comprised only about 30 percent of the student body. In the same way that the Girl Scout plays Irena wrote criticized the existing order, this study presented a subtle criticism of the growing privileges of Poland's elite.

Critiques of the government grew sharper in the following years. In 1965, for the first time, Irena witnessed the risks of taking such a course. Kuron and another professor, Karol Modzelewski, wrote an open letter to the Polish Party in which they presented the argument that the Gomulka government violated several Marxist principles. The letter found its way into the hands of American radicals and was published in the United States by a Trotskyite group. The two were arrested and tried under a Polish law that makes a person liable for spreading false economic and political information and for collaborating with foreign enemies. Irena helped collect signatures on a petition in defense of her friends. Within days more than one thousand signatures were gathered. For the first time since 1956 there emerged a group, however loosely formed, in open opposition to the government.

The court found the two professors guilty. They were each sentenced to three and a half years in prison. In addition, two students who organized the petition drive were suspended from the university. Kuron's conviction only strengthened Irena's belief that the government needed revision.

The convictions and suspensions exacerbated tensions on campus. Between 1965 and 1967, the student body split into two distinct factions: the Socialist Youth, who fully supported government actions, and informally organized discussion groups composed of those who had been infulenced by Kuron and Modzelewski.

Irena grew closer to the center of dissident activities. The students engaged in extended analysis of Polish society from a neo-Marxist point of view, a position outlined in *The New Class* by Yugoslav dissident Milovan Djilas. The more they talked the more convinced Irena became that the government needed serious reform.

In January 1967, Irena and nine of her friends were told by the police that their discussion group was not sanctioned by the university nor by the government and therefore had no right to exist. They were told to disband.

"We were only a theoretical discussion group. But this was considered threatening. The state had its undercover agents; some of the students were employed by the state, so they knew all about what we were doing."

Shortly after the students received the warning, Kuron and Modzelewski were released from prison, having served a reduced sentence because they had no previous record. While they were not rehired by the university, they did spend much of their time around the campus and became the focal point of the discussion groups, which continued despite the government's warning. The two professors dominated the political forums, lending their intellectual weight to the groups. As they were folk heroes of a sort, most of the discussions revolved around their critique.

Emboldened by the upsurge of student protest throughout Europe, the dissident students in Warsaw decided to meet more regularly. Until then the groups had formed more or less spontaneously. Now they organized themselves into units of about fifty students each to gather at monthly meetings. Since these groups were not authorized and had been discouraged by the government, they could not publicly state the reason for their getting together. But neither could they meet secretly, since a group that size would attract government spies. Under the pretext of getting together for birthday parties, the groups began to meet throughout Warsaw to apply a Marxist critique to the existing government.

"It was a kind of Marxist revisionism. By this time I was no longer a committed Marxist myself. I found too many inconsistencies in it. At that time, I was working on my doctoral dissertation and the goal of my thesis was to point out these inconsistencies.

"The Marxist system is so pervasive—in the judicial system, in the political system, in the schools, in practically every sphere of life—that it was very hard to challenge it from the outside. The only thing you could do was to take over the same slogans as the Marxists and try to prove that the existing regime was not Marxist enough."

Anti-American demonstrations aimed against the Vietnam War took place on many European campuses by October that year. While students at Warsaw University also felt strongly against American participation in Southeast Asia, they seized this as a chance to present their views of Polish life in a public forum without confronting the state head-on.

"We decided to have a demonstration which we would use for our own purposes. We decided to rally in favor of the Vietnamese people, supporting their right to self-determination. We were against American intervention in the country, so on one level our protest was acceptable. But at the same time we offered an analysis of Poland, Hungary, and Czechoslovakia in terms of self-determination. We made a link between Vietnamese oppression by the Americans and Polish oppression by the Russians. Our rally was double-edged. Because of the Anti-American element it was very difficult for the state to suppress it."

Kuron and Modzelewski did not agree with the student's tactics. They remembered well their time in prison and were sobered by that experience. They told the students that the state had limits of tolerance. Irena listened but, full of youthful vigor and buoyed by student successes elsewhere, chose to ignore their caution.

Some minor incidents followed. As dissident students handed out leaflets around campus, a few scuffles broke out. Members of the Socialist Youth grabbed the leaflets and with the police attempted to confiscate them. There were no serious injuries, no one was suspended, and there were no arrests. The students had won a small victory.

Dissident students were not alone in their attempt to liberalize government policies and in their attitudes towards Polish self-determination. A Warsaw theater group revived a well-known nineteenth-century play, *The Forefathers,* by Adam Mickiewicu. Because of its anti-Russian theme, the play had always been popular with Polish nationalists. Although Mickiewicu's plays and poems were well-known throughout Poland, his works had been discouraged by the pro-Russian government since World War II.

The play was produced in January 1968. Anti-Russian lines in the play received applause from the audience on several nights. The Ministry of Culture and Art banned the production.

Irena and her group discussed the ban and decided to demonstrate on behalf of the play and against censorship. They prepared placards and on the night of the play's final performance picketed the theater, denouncing censorship and supporting the theater workshop.

The play finished around midnight. The students decided to make a final show by marching through the dark streets to a statue of Mickiewicu. Carrying signs, chanting slogans, they went through the deserted night streets, a band of noisy students on a cold winter night.

When they reached the statue, they made a few short speeches and placed wreaths of flowers at the foot of the playwright. It had been a long night. They were tired and cold.

"We wanted to go home then. But we couldn't. We had not noticed it before, but now when we looked around we saw a cordon of police cars. The street was dark and quiet. We no longer shouted our slogans and began to walk away from the square. As we walked, the police followed us very slowly in their cars."

The cars stopped, the police got out and began arresting the students, taking them into their cars. Apparently, the police had not anticipated so many demonstrators—there were more students to be arrested than places in the cars. The police picked up all they could. Fortunately for Irena, there was no more room for her, and she was allowed to walk home.

The next morning all those arrested were released but seven received fines. Irena believes that each of those fined was singled out for a particular purpose. "Two of them were the leaders of our march, two others had parents who were not in good stead with the Party. The other three I think were fined because they were Jews."

That year the Polish government had taken a hard line against Zionism, often implying that Jews were enemies of the state. Poles with Jewish names were being purged from the Party and removed from government posts. Comments by world Jewish community leaders expressed fear of a new round of anti-Semitism.

It never occurred to Irena that the anti-Zionist policy would touch her.

With the march against censorship, Irena took an increasingly larger part in plans for further activities. Despite police warnings and tightening censorship, the students decided to step up their protests. They printed new leaflets in defense of *The Forefathers* and distributed them throughout campus.

"We knew that what we were doing was illegal. There is an administration rule which says that the publication of a piece of more than fifty copies must be approved by the government censorship office. We didn't seek approval and we printed more than fifty copies. But we felt that what we were doing was legal under the provision of the Polish constitution which allows for freedom of publication. So we took our chances."

Since the printing facilities of the dissidents were limited, they managed to print only a few hundred pamphlets. The Socialist Youth retaliated with thousands of leaflets.

"It was clear that their leaflets were promoted by the secret police. They were well-organized, and their pamphlets followed the official anti-Zionist line of the government. It was the same anti-Semitism which had been promoted since the Six Day War, less than a year before."

The students countered with a new set of leaflets. It was then that they noticed that they were under constant surveillance.

"The police started following us. We didn't know if they wanted to provoke us into doing something so they would have an excuse to arrest us, or if they wanted to prevent us from taking some action. We had no way of knowing which it was, so we continued to follow the course we planned. When I left in the morning, there would be two cars following me. If I went to the park, two men would get out and walk behind me. They went everywhere I went."

The students dropped the pretense of holding birthday parties. Now Irena led open meetings critical of the government. A petition was drawn up supporting *The Forefathers* and condemning censorship. The university administration responded by suspending two students for having collected signatures for the petition. The students were suspended summarily, without a hearing, which university procedures required.

Over Kuron's objection, the students countered by announcing a rally to be held at the university's main square on May 8. Because of her intensity and articulateness, Irena was chosen to give the opening speech.

The suspension of the two students had galvanized the Warsaw students into action. The turnout of nearly 4,000 students surprised even Irena and the organizers. The square was jammed. Others stood by windows at buildings around the plaza. Some circulated throughout the crowd collecting signatures. About 3,000 students affixed their names. Waving placards, the students began chanting We Want *The Forefathers!* and No Bread Without Freedom!

While the students chanted and cheered, buses full of Volunteer Workers Militia, organized by the government, parked at the edge of the campus. The workers began to move around the fringe of the crowd, yelling slogans of their own: Students Return To Work! We Work, They Study, We Want Calm! For several years there had been antagonism between workers and students, with workers derisively terming the students "banana children," i.e., people privileged enough to afford bananas.

Some workers, brandishing clubs, began to hit and kick some students, punching them to the ground. The students, schooled in passive resistance, went limp, refusing to engage in violence.

At this point, Irena climbed on a bench to read the resolution that the students had drawn up. As she began, the Socialist Youth and workers tried to shout her down. Some students shouted back.

"But we didn't let anyone provoke us into violence—not the Socialist Youth nor the Militia. We wanted to engage in passive disobedience."

Over the verbal melee, Irena read the resolution. It stated their support for the Polish Constitution, especially Chapter 7, which guaranteed the right to assembly, free speech, and press. On that basis they opposed the banning of *The Forefathers.* They demanded that the suspended students be reinstated and ended by supporting the liberalization policies then taking place in Czechoslovakia.

When Irena finished, the students sat down in the square, waiting. The university rector sent word to the student leaders that he was willing to meet with a delegation.

"When we got up to the rector's office, I had the impression that he really wasn't interested in meeting with us. I had the feeling that he was stalling for time, that he was putting us off. He didn't get right down to things. Instead he suggested that we could talk more reasonably if we came back the next day, after matters had cooled down."

The rector asked Irena to address the students in the square outside his office. She could use the balcony of his office and tell the students that he had agreed to meet with them the following day. Irena thought that his proposal was fair and agreed to it.

"As I stepped out onto the balcony, I could see buses full of riot police arriving. The police got out and began beating the students. The students hadn't done anything. They were sitting there peacefully. I'd say there were about three hundred police in addition to the Workers Militia. Together they clubbed the students. The doors to all the buildings were locked. The students started running. From the balcony I could see this mayhem, students running, crying, the police beating them. This must have lasted for about an hour."

A faculty member concerned with Irena's safety led her through an underground passage across campus. When Irena emerged from the tunnel, she found herself in a church full of students who escaped from the square, some wounded and bleeding.

Irena managed to reach her apartment safely. Later that evening a friend phoned to tell her that he thought Kuron had been arrested. Also, fifteen members of her discussion group were missing.

Rumors circulated throughout Warsaw that night that a student had been killed during the riot. In the Party's official newspaper the next morning, the only mention of the riot was a denial that a student had been killed. No explanation was given regarding the government's action at the university.

Irena's brother visited her the morning after the riot. He left but immediately returned to warn her that the police were downstairs. There was a knock at the door. Plainclothes police entered her apartment and very politely, without asking questions, told her to come with them.

The police treated her courteously in the car, offering her a cigarette, for which, as a chain-smoker, Irena was grateful. Once inside the police station they began questioning her.

"The person who interrogated me the first day wasn't very intelligent. He seemed as though he didn't know what to ask. For instance, he wanted to know why I was at the university, who told me about the various meetings, and so on. I didn't want to refuse to answer, so I replied in a non-commital way. I had the impression that he didn't even know that I had spoken at the rally."

Irena was unaware of continued protests on the street that day. Warsaw University had become the site of a massive rally, with as many as 10,000 people—students and non-students—gathered to show their support for the students' cause. Rallies were held at other universities throughout Poland and the building of the Ministry of Culture and Art was sacked by a group demonstrating there.

All that day the police hunted for students throughout Warsaw, taking them from their apartments, beating them, and bringing them to jail. In less than a week, nearly 1,000 students were arrested.

On March 10, two days after the demonstration, Irena was taken to Hooligan Court, the judiciary body responsible for misdemeanors and other minor crimes. There they read to Irena the charge for which she was arraigned: standing on a public bench with dirty shoes.

The court cited student shouts of "Gestapo" as evidence that the students had insulted the police. Furthermore, one policeman testified that he saw Irena on the rector's balcony motioning with her hands to the students below. For this she was accused of having provoked a riot. When Irena asked him what sort of motions he referred to, the policeman remained silent.

Irena had no legal representation. There was no appealing the court's decision. Within ten minutes, she was sentenced to two months in jail.

"They brought me to the basement of the police headquarters. I didn't know what they wanted to do with me. I became quite frightened at this point. In a short while a plainclothesman came and took me to a huge auditorium full of riot police in full battle gear. As I was taken through the auditorium, one policeman looked at me and said, 'This is the bitch I saw yesterday at the university.' He began to move toward me but the plainclothesman said to him, 'No, you don't touch her.' I think the government didn't want to be charged with physical brutality, so he stopped him."

She was brought to Warsaw's Rakoviecka Prison, where she was questioned nearly every day, sometimes as long as twelve hours per day. Irena wanted to know why they were questioning her since she had already received her sentence. They told her that they had nothing against her, that the questioning had to do with the activities of others. They only wanted her to answer their questions.

"They assured me that nothing could happen to me since I wasn't accused of a crime. I was simply arrested for hooliganism. But they said they wanted me to testify at the trials of other students and as a witness I was legally required to answer their questions. This was very clever. If I had been accused of a crime, then I would have the right to refuse to answer questions which would be self-incriminating. But as a witness I had to answer."

She resorted to fabrication. When the police realized that her answers were worthless, they changed her status to accused. She was charged with belonging to a secret organization whose aim was the overthrow of the government. If guilty, she would serve between six months and fifteen years. With such an indefinite sentence, the police thought they could bargain for her cooperation.

Irena's cell was small but she felt fortunate compared to conditions under which many male students were kept. "You could hear sounds from cell to cell and I could sometimes hear screams coming from one. I assumed they were being beaten. They were more subtle with me. They implied that a good friend of mine had been arrested and my cooperation would make things easier for him. But this had the opposite effect upon me. It made me stronger by making me angry."

Punishments were given to Irena frequently. The prison authorities found many reasons to punish her. They accused her of not making her bed properly. For this they rescinded her right to receive packages. Violating another prison regulation resulted in her losing the right to correspondence. Another time they took away her cigarette privileges.

At one point the interrogation officer told her that he would no longer try to extract information from her. He said that if she wanted to offer any information she should let him know.

The next day she was sent to the punishment cell. "This was in the basement. The windows didn't close, and it was very cold.

There was no mattress. The toilets didn't work, and there was a stench. But I was allowed to bring books with me, so I read in the dim light. Within two days I became very sick. I had an ulcer. When I first reported it, they thought I was lying. But the day after my stomach grew worse. They gave me some injections for it. This made me even sicker. So they finally took me from the punishment cell and returned me upstairs. When my interrogation officer saw what happened, he said to me, 'I told you, any time you want to talk just call me up.' "

A few weeks after the demonstration, Gomulka addressed the nation about the student unrest. He singled out Irena as one of the student leaders, referring to her as Irena Lasota Hirszowicz. Then he moved away from his prepared text and added, "There were two others—our students, you know, Poles—who spoke."

Gomulka's comment was echoed in the Party newspaper, which described the demonstration in such a way as to give the impression that most student leaders were Jewish. Jozef Kepa, Party Secretary for Warsaw, accused Zionists of organizing the riots. Workers in the Foreign Trade Ministry passed a resolution demanding that authorities "stop tolerating the activity of reactionary Zionist elements." The communist leader of Silesia district repeated that Zionists were pitting students against workers. He went on to blame most of Poland's economic difficulties upon Zionists. The government also dismissed three high officials who were fathers of demonstrators. All three were Jews.

In prison, the authorities continued to punish Irena. One time she spent a week in the punishment cell; another time ten days.

"In some ways my worst punishment was my cell mate. She talked incessantly. I couldn't stand it anymore. So once when I was caught talking to another inmate through my window, I asked them to send me to the punishment cell. I think she must have been a government spy sent there to torment me."

The police used another approach to intimidate Irena. When she missed her period—a common experience for women under stress—she went to the prison doctor. The doctor insisted she was pregnant and was going to perform an abortion without anaesthesia. Irena protested that she was not pregnant. The doctor finally gave her an injection to regularize her menstruation.

Irena believes that the police were not interested in obtaining information. Their intent was to gain confessions and have the students denounce each other. Irena was given a letter allegedly written by a friend asking Irena to cooperate with the police as a means of helping Kuron. Her friend wrote that all there was to know about their group had already appeared in the newspapers. The best way to help Kuron would be to testify. That way she could explain that Kuron was not involved in planning the demonstration. While the letter sounded reasonable to Irena, she disregarded it. She felt that the authorities did not know everything. Later, Irena learned that her friend had received a similar letter from another friend. The letters were forgeries, most likely the work of the police.

The police were counting on Irena's friendship with Kuron to make her testify. But Irena never offered any information.

"One of the reasons I resisted the interrogations so well is that soon after my detention I began to read newspapers and saw the extent of the demonstrations. I was sure that I would get a three-year sentence. It seemed obvious to me that I would be spending that time in prison anyhow, so I was swayed very little by the police officers."

When Irena's two month's detention expired, she was not released. They continued to hold her, this time to await trial on the new charges of belonging to a subversive organization.

The Gomulka government was shaken by the extensive demonstrations. In an attempt to mollify some of its opponents, the government decided against holding one large trial for all the students. Instead, in late July it released Irena in her own recognizance.

But the government had not dropped its plan to try the dissidents. Kuron was accused of treason. The state's major contention was that he had given information regarding the student demonstration to foreign correspondents. He was found guilty.

Some male students were drafted into the army and others were sent to labor camps for periods of from two to six months.

The government set Irena's trial for April 1969. This was to be the last of a series of trials involving dissidents. When the government began the trials, it had a difficult time proving the existence of a dissident organization. It had to produce evidence regarding membership, and this it could not do. No such list existed. The government went on to establish its case on two grounds. First, while the organization did not exist as an entity, nevertheless it did exist objectively. Second, the organization was so secret that the members themselves were unaware of its existence.

The first two defendants were sentenced to three years each. Once the guilt of these individuals was established, subsequent trials were easier, since they were made adjuncts to the first.

When Irena's case reached court, she received an eighteen-month sentence, which she appealed. She was allowed to remain out of jail, confined to Warsaw, while awaiting a new trial.

In July, Poland celebrated its twenty-fifth anniversary as a republic. The government used this occasion to offer a general amnesty to everyone with less than two years to serve.

Ironically, it was the government's anti-Zionist campaign which permitted Irena to leave Poland. During the year after the demonstrations, half of Poland's 25,000 Jews left the country, an emigration encouraged by the state. The government approached Irena and suggested she apply for an exit visa as a person of Jewish origin.

For six months she was kept under constant surveillance. Then in 1970, with visa in hand, she arrived in the United States.

Postscript: Kuron, spokesperson for the Social Self-Defense Committee, was arrested while on holiday on August 18, 1978. Police informed him that he would not be allowed to remain at the Baltic resort and accompanied him back to Warsaw.

On November 15, 1978, while on his way to give a lecture on "Education and Social Life," Kuron was arrested in Warsaw. Police occupied his apartment in which the lecture was to have taken place and detained five people as they arrived.

Kuron was prevented from giving a lecture at his apartment on January 25, 1979, by a group of unidentified individuals. The lecture formed part of a course in sociology in the second term of the Society of Academic Courses.

Despite police harassment, the Social Self-Defense Committee continued its activities, developing into one of the strongest dissident groups in Poland. In addition to its lecture series, it published several underground journals. It also established links with Polish workers, providing many with a philosophical basis for their growing demands for autonomy.

In August 1980, numerous strikes hit Polish factories and shipyards. The Committee was singled out by the Communist Party for its part in the disruptions. Later that month, Kuron and seventeen others were detained by the government.

In September, the Polish workers' conditions were met. Kuron was released. However, by mid-September the Polish media once again criticized the dissidents, in particular Kuron, calling him an "anti-socialist enemy of the state."

Steven Wabunoha

Uganda

No one shall be arbitrarily deprived of his property.
> *Article 17, section 2, Universal*
> *Declaration of Human Rights*

Called the Pearl of Africa by Winston Churchill, Uganda, the country at the Nile's headwaters, was ruled by the British from the late nineteenth century until 1962. In that year, this landlocked country, consisting of more than thirty ethnic groups and nearly as many languages, gained its independence.

When Milton Obote became the country's first Prime Minister, he inherited a government severely divided along ethnic lines, with four long-established kingdoms attempting to maintain traditional control. By 1964, the alliance between Obote and one of the strongest kings was severed. The country was thrown into turmoil, and in 1966 the kingdom of Buganda attempted to secede from the country. Obote responded with a military attack on the king's palace. Political arrests and suppression of dissent soon followed.

In order to maintain his position of power, Obote strengthened the military under the leadership of Idi Amin. As Obote's popularity waned, Amin's grew.

While Obote was attending the Commonwealth Conference in Singapore in January 1971, Idi Amin moved his troops into Kampala and seized the reins of government.

NOT ALL POLITICAL PRISONERS are dissidents. Often it is enough for a government to merely perceive an individual as a threat to its existence, even if that threat is as benign as the possession of a telephone. This was true in the case of Steven Wabunoha of Uganda.

"In 1977, several men from the PSU (Public Safety Unit) visited me and wanted to know about my portable telephone. I told them I bought it in England on a business trip. That was the truth. But they accused me of working for the CIA. They said I had it because I was listening in on President Amin and that I was a spy."

Steven knew that from that point on his fate rested with the PSU. There would be no civil trial, no fair and open hearing, no defense counsel, no judge. Such niceties had evaporated years before in Uganda.

Steven had not spoken out against the government, he belonged to no political or cultural groups that could be viewed as opposition. In fact, Steven tacitly supported the Amin regime, for during its reign of power he had become a successful businessman.

However, he now realized that the power of the police had turned against him. He believed that by the next morning he would be in a mass grave or simply dumped as a corpse in a nearby river. By this time Steven knew that Uganda did not keep political prisoners. It simply murdered them.

1971: Like hundreds of thousands of other Ugandans, Steven welcomed the coup that toppled President Milton Obote. Eighteen-year-old Steven looked forward to a change of government. Many Ugandans were tired of political factions, corruption, a sluggish economy, and the broken promises of freedom.

"When Amin came to power, we thought this was going to be a better government, a better life for the people."

Very few realized that Uganda would soon be transformed into a state of terror. During the next eight years, nearly one in every twenty citizens would be either jailed, forced into exile, or murdered.

"When he came he made many promises to us: tax cuts, freedom of speech, freedom of everything."

Amin's idea of freedom was soon implemented. One month after the coup, Idi Amin abolished Parliament, suspended all political parties, and enacted rule by presidential decree.

Acting under Decree No. 7, which empowered security forces "to detain indefinitely without charge any person suspected of subversion," about eight hundred officers from the army, police, and secret service of former President Obote were arrested.

In Malire, thirty-two soldiers suspected of supporting Obote were killed; scores of soldiers in the Mbarara barracks and in the barracks in Jinja were executed; thirty-four soldiers were shot or slashed to death in Makindye barracks; the president of the Industrial Court was shot and his body burnt in a Kampala suburb; two Americans—a freelance journalist and a sociology lecturer at Makerere University in Kampala—were murdered after inquiring about the deaths of the soldiers in Mbarara.

Steven was surprised by the violent events. Uganda, unlike neighboring Kenya, had not experienced a revolution for independence, so perhaps, Steven thought, this was the price that now had to be paid for true freedom. Besides, as far as Steven knew, the events were only rumors circulating in an unstable environment. Only later would the incidents be documented.

Steven had had nothing to do with the Obote government. He could remain safely on the sidelines.

In May, four months after the coup, the violence touched Steven's family.

"I had an uncle who was the head of pediatrics in Mbare. He was planning to get married. A few days before the wedding he got a telephone call from someone who said he was from the army. He told my uncle that if he married this woman my uncle would suffer the consequences.

"My uncle was frightened by the call. He decided to talk to the base commander himself. The commander assured him that there was nothing to worry about. So my uncle married. After his honeymoon, he returned. Early one morning some soldiers came to his house and collected him. Nobody ever saw him again."

Steven and several of his relatives went to the commander to inquire about their uncle's whereabouts. The commander denied any knowledge of the incident.

Still Steven was not frightened. His uncle was a big man, a prominent person. Steven was a small man. The government would not bother with him. He felt safe.

1972: In August, President Amin announced that in a dream God had directed him to expel Uganda's 50,000 Asians. He gave them ninety days to leave the country or find themselves "sitting on the fire." Although many foreign governments voiced their concern, within Uganda the move against the Asians was a popular one. Since the Asians comprised the bulk of Uganda's mercantile class, spoke Indian dialects which were incomprehensible to the Africans, and had arrived with the British colonials at the turn of the century, many Ugandans welcomed their departure. It was viewed as the final blow against colonialism. The fact that 20,000 Indians were Ugandan citizens seemed to make little difference.

"Amin's saying that businesses should go to Ugandans was not a bad thing. But the way it was done was bad. It was just grabbing and hitting. The Asians weren't allowed to take even a spoon with them; they had to go without money. It was just inhuman."

Thousands of shops were vacated by November. Although the government's method of expropriating Asian property left a bad taste in Steven's mouth, when allocation committees were established to distribute shops to Africans, Steven and an uncle applied for one. Since his uncle had business experience and Steven had attended two years of college, the committee granted them a dry goods shop. At an unspecified date in the future, they would pay the government its fair value. At the moment the government was less concerned about collecting money than keeping the economy going.

As the allocation procedures deteriorated into a system of nepotism, Steven benefited from the chaos.

"Making money was easy for us in that situation. Since shops were being given to people without experience, there really wasn't any competition. We were among the few who knew how to run a business. The production of local fabrics became unreliable, so I had to make frequent trips to Kenya to buy some there. I went to England one time to buy fabric. That is when I bought the telephone."

1972–1973: Death became a common feature of daily life. At times the Nile River was choked with bloated bodies.

Uganda publicly exhibited a group of alleged terrorists. A military tribunal sat in secret session for one day. For the first time in the twentieth century, there was a public execution in Uganda. President Amin invited parents and relatives of the twelve victims to watch the execution by firing squad.

Steven realized that he needed to take steps to protect himself.

"Our lives were becoming like the life of a drunkard's chicken. You know that at any time you can die. Anytime for no reason you can go, for nothing, just because some army man doesn't like you."

Since the military seemed to wield most of the power, Steven cultivated a friend within its ranks. He hoped that if he were unjustly attacked by the military he would be able to turn to his friend for protection.

Uganda had become a country run by collectives of thugs, a kind of African Mafia with semi-independent gangs loyal to Idi Amin. The government had been replaced by gangsters.

Steven's friend could offer only limited protection; he could not serve as his personal bodyguard. Twice that year Steven was beaten by the police: once, near Kampala, when he was found driving without his registration and another time, near Jinja, when a soldier found the photo on Steven's registration had been placed horizontally instead of vertically.

1974: All foreign newspapers were banned. President Amin's recently divorced wife was arrested, and her dismembered body was found several days later. Idi Amin announced a park would be named in honor of Adolf Hitler.

1975: Steven's friend told him that the government had opened files on nearly everyone, and, while his file was still clean, there was cause for concern. Under the Economic Tribunal Decree of March 25, crimes such as overcharging, smuggling, and corruption were punishable by death and were to be judged by military courts.

"He told me they knew I had a car and did business in Kenya. I wanted to know what they thought I might be doing wrong. He didn't know. He sipped his beer and told me to be careful."

It did not take Steven long to find out the hold the military had over him. One night on the way home from his shop he was stopped by a plainclothes officer. After polite questioning, the officer ordered Steven to take him to his house whereupon he searched the premises.

"He wanted to know how much money I had and demanded that I pay him a large sum of money. He said he would report me if I didn't pay it to him.

"I didn't have any money in the house to give him. I told him my uncle had all the cash. He allowed me to see my uncle and warned me not to play any tricks on him. I went to my uncle but told him I wasn't sure I wanted to give the soldier the money. My uncle told me not to be foolish. He said if I refused I would be killed. He was probably right, so I paid the money."

First extortion, then theft. Steven was pulled to the roadside by a police car. The policeman did not want Steven's registration. He wanted the car keys. Steven gave them to him and never saw his car again.

1976: An attempt was made on Amin's life. A student at Makerere University was killed by the PSU. The chairman of the inquiry into the student's death was expelled. Two of Amin's sons were sent to prison.

1977: In order to respond to the deteriorating economic situation, the government amended the anti-smuggling decree of 1975. The new version read that "any person who diverts certain commodities to unscheduled destinations, even within Uganda, faces death by firing squad."

The major food supplier to Makerere University was arrested. He disappeared and was presumed dead. Several senior bank officials were arrested and given prison sentences. Many business people were arrested or missing.

Steven witnessed an abduction by the police.

"It was midday, broad daylight, not far from my shop. A car came speeding along and went in front of another car to stop it. Two people walked to the first car and pulled somebody out. He started yelling for help. We all knew who this man was. He was the chief librarian at the university. Lots of us watched this happen but nobody could move."

The abandoned car remained on the traffic circle for days. No one dared approach it. Finally, the police towed it away.

Steven also witnessed beatings on the street.

"I saw people beaten who had been shot. I once found a body in a stream in Kampala. There were bullet wounds all over. Everybody stopped to look. We watched until the army drove up and took it away. I was frightened, really scared. But I got used to hearing about killings and seeing bodies. I got used to it."

What he could not get used to was the harassment. In September he arrived at his shop to find a PSU car in front and his clerk sitting in the middle of the floor surrounded by uniformed men. All the shelves had been emptied and the men were stacking the goods in a corner.

They told him that they had reason to believe that the goods were smuggled and that they were taking him and the goods to Naguru Police Training School, the PSU headquarters. But they never reached Naguru. Instead, they told him to return to his shop and appear at Naguru the next day with his receipts. If he could prove that the cloth had been gotten properly, it would be returned to him.

The next morning Steven went to Naguru, receipts in hand, expecting his merchandise to be returned. He went from desk to desk trying to locate someone who knew about the goods. He was finally ordered out and he left because he knew that to persist would be risky. They might detain him.

Upon returning to Kampala, Steven contacted his friend. This was, after all, why he had this friendship. He wanted the cloth back. He had the PSU car number and described the men to his friend.

"He told me to forget it. He said he could find the men for me, but if action were taken against them they would find a way of getting to me. The moment I tried to recover the cloth I'd no longer be living."

Steven could well believe that death would be forthcoming. His friend could no longer protect him, just as the church could no longer protect its clergy. Early in the year the Ugandan bishops issued a protest against killings, disappearances, abuses of power, and harassment of church people by security forces. They were summoned to meet with Amin. During the meeting the Archbishop was arrested. The following day the government announced that he and two cabinet ministers, who were also arrested that day, had died in a car accident as they attempted escape.

During the next few weeks, according to several diplomatic sources, as many as 10,000 people were killed by government troops. In September, twelve senior government officials were publicly executed.

Reports about beatings to death by hammer appeared. According to Amnesty International, a private house in Kampala was the scene of more than two hundred deaths by bludgeoning.

It was in this atmosphere that Steven faced arrest for possession of his telephone. He knew that he would probably not leave Naguru alive.

"I told them I didn't know I needed permission to have such a telephone. They wanted to know where I kept it. I told them it was at my house, so they drove me there. I showed it to them, hoping they would be reasonable, that they would confiscate the phone and leave me.

"They told me I had to go to jail. I asked what for. They said for the telephone. I wasn't authorized to buy one. I told them I wasn't trying to hide it. But they insisted that I intended to tap the messages of the president."

They took Steven to a section of Naguru used for interrogation, detention, and torture. As they led him downstairs to a room for questioning, he heard screams in the corridors, saw people being beaten in the hallways, heard sobs and pleas for mercy. People were being led from room to room, holding their wounds, trailing blood, clutching their injuries.

As soon as Steven was placed in a room, the police took a three foot long coaxial cable and whipped him across the head. They accused him of working against the president. They wanted to know which revolutionary groups he belonged to, who else was plotting with him to overthrow the government. They wanted to know why he owned the telephone, who else he spoke to, where he bought it, what kind of business he was in.

He was beaten on the back, flogged with the cable until he bled. They slapped him across the face and kicked him.

After nearly an hour, they removed him from the room and brought him to a cell.

"When I was beaten I was alone. Then afterwards I was put with about twenty-five people in a cell the size of a kitchen. Many of them were beaten very badly, much worse than me. Some were swollen. Others couldn't stand."

Meanwhile, Steven's wife learned from the shop clerk that the PSU had taken Steven from the shop. She immediately contacted his army friend to see what he might know. The soldier surmised that Steven had been taken to Naguru, and he advised her to get a large sum of money to give to him. She had no choice but to trust him. He explained that he would go to Naguru himself and attempt to bribe some people.

Steven slept fitfully that night. His body was sore. The moaning of other prisoners kept him awake. He anticipated a morning execution.

Early the next morning the cell door opened. There, instead of the jailer, was his friend. His friend whispered, "Get out of here quickly. You know what's going to happen to you."

Steven left Naguru. Afraid of returning home, he went downtown.

"I was the most frightened person. Even when I walked out of there I thought they would follow me. I think they didn't because they were really after my property, my shop. They knew I wasn't a spy. They could have everything they wanted without killing me. They even got some bribe money out of it."

Steven told his friend where he was going; the soldier contacted his wife and in a short while she met him in Kampala. She persuaded Steven to leave Uganda.

"She said it was no good for me to stay. My life would be going soon. I didn't want to go but she argued with me. She told me she would arrange matters and she and my children would meet me in Kenya as soon as possible."

Although the country was in a near state of collapse, some services still operated sporadically. Steven paid his fare on a taxi station wagon that ran from Kampala to the Kenyan border, a hundred miles to the east.

The border, which a few years before had been an open one, now was heavily patroled to control smuggling and the flow of refugees. Every vehicle and person was thoroughly searched. Since Steven had crossed the border many times on business, he knew how to comport himself. This meant answering questions correctly and offering bribes to the right people. He presented his business papers, claiming that he intended to buy some fabric for his shop. He paid his bribes.

They let him cross the border without incident.

In Kampala, the PSU confiscated his house, forcing his wife and children to move into her father's house. After four months of preparation, his wife and children joined him in Nairobi, Kenya.

1978: The Wabunoha family settled in the United States.

"There were many people who were involved in trying to get rid of Amin. But personally, I didn't care. The only thing I cared about was my work, my business doing okay. Otherwise, I didn't care. Even when other people disappeared, I thought about it, but it never occurred to me that I would be in so much danger. When I was in trouble, that's when I started realizing that things were really terrible. Each time the police came to me—when they took my car, when they took my money, when they took my cloth—I thought that then they had everything they wanted so they wouldn't bother me again.

"I felt bad when Amin chased the Asians out of the country. But I still took the business. I knew that it was a bad system with everyone disappearing, but I didn't try to do something about it. You didn't know who to trust. Anyone could have been a spy and told the army about your not liking the government. So I just kept quiet about these things. The way I feel now is that I'd like to go back and clean up the mess. But before I was arrested that never occurred to me."

1979: Steven joined a group of Ugandan exiles in the United States. He was plotting the intended assassination of President Amin when the combined forces of Tanzania and Ugandan exiles in East Africa toppled the regime.

Charito Planas

Philippines

Everyone has the right to take part in the government of his country, directly or through freely chosen representatives.
Article 21, Universal Declaration
of Human Rights

The only Christian country in Asia, the Philippines was ruled as a Spanish colony for nearly four hundred years and as an American colony for slightly less than half a century.

As the war in Southeast Asia intensified in the 1960s, the American military presence in the Philippines grew. The country became a major base for American supplies and planes used in Vietnam. The war in Vietnam drew worldwide criticism and anti-American sentiment increased in the Philippines. In the early 1970s, as feeling against U.S. corporations and military bases grew, the Philippine Congress passed a law limiting foreign ownership of business and land. It appeared to many observers that the Philippine Supreme Court was nearing a decision that would enable the government to confiscate much American-owned property.

It was in this context that President Ferdinand Marcos declared martial law in September 1972.

76

IN THE PHILIPPINES' FIRST ELECTION in six years, two candidates were squared against each other for a seat in the newly created National Assembly. One, a former beauty queen, was Imelda Marcos, Governor of Metropolitan Manila and wife of President Ferdinand Marcos. The other was Charito Planas, Director of the Philippine Chamber of Commerce, a round-faced woman who often jokes about her plumpness.

In one part of Manila, Imelda arrived in a black limousine surrounded by scores of security forces, cheerleaders, and movie stars. The state-controlled TV covered the rally. While sandwiches and drinks were being given away to the audience, the First Lady told them, "I can tell the President what you need. You know that Imelda always gets action."

In another part of the city, Charito stood on top of an oil drum to address the crowd. She held up an enlarged photograph of the President's wife and, pointing to a diamond tiara, said, "This crown is worth 10 million pesos. Do you know what you can do with 10 million pesos? We could build 1,000 houses for the poor. Look at her earrings. They are worth 200 houses. Her ring has a diamond as big as an egg. That's 2,000 houses. Her bracelet is worth 200 houses. She just sits there, wearing these things for her own pleasure.

"She says that she is for the people. Why doesn't she give her jewelry away? And her vanity! She changes her clothes several times a day for no reason. New clothes for here, different clothes for there. She travels around the world and puts up at expensive hotels. All for her vanity. But there's nothing for the squatters."

To counter the opposition's growing appeal, President Marcos addressed the nation on television. He accused Laban, the opposition party, of "sowing discord, hate, confusion and resentment." He went on to call Laban's candidates "strong and willing handmaidens" to the Communists.

Charito lashed back. "The government calls us subversives. They call the people who loved their country and gave their lives for it subversives. But I call those in the administration subversives. They have taken away our liberties. I accuse the administration of robbing the treasury and amassing wealth at the expense of the people. They call us traitors; they say that the opposition are traitors to the government. But I say that they are the real traitors.

They have betrayed the cause of freedom, they have betrayed the squatters, they have betrayed the laborers. It is they who are traitors."

She ended the rally by calling upon the crowd to let President Marcos hear their voices. With upraised fists they responded: "Laban! Laban! (Fight! Fight!)"

Charito knew very well the risk she was running in her criticism of the government; she realized that this probably would be the end of her political freedom. "My language was very strong. I knew what I was doing. I understood the consequences."

This was April 1978. And it was not the first time that Charito faced detention. Soon after the Japanese occupation of the Philippines, Charito, her older sister, Carmen, and her mother were imprisoned. Charito was not yet a teenager.

"I grew up in an atmosphere of concern. I knew about social justice very well because I worked with my sister Carmen on her campaigns beginning in 1939, when she was elected as the first woman to the Manila City Council. After the war, Carmen resumed her political activities, and I was always at her side. I saw how she served people. Most importantly, she taught me how to have convictions and to fight for them no matter what the cost."

By the time Carmen died in 1964, Charito had acquired a reputation of her own. She was invited to national and international conferences on education, social work, law, and business. She also participated in several trade missions to promote Philippine business.

After attending a conference on pre-school education held in Washington, D.C., in the late 1960s, she began a kindergarten in her garage for the children of neighboring poor people. Although she lived in an exclusive residential area in Quezon City, there were pockets of squatters between the well-kept houses. At first there was no charge for the school. "But I saw how this was sort of demeaning, so I charged a token fee which was almost like not charging at all. I explained to them that it was better that we were on equal terms rather than my giving them a dole. The school was very successful and the idea spread." Several more kindergartens were established in squatter areas and by 1978 more than 4,000 had graduated from them.

Charito was also an active member of the Red Cross. During

one major flood, she directed relief activity by distributing food and clothing to flood victims. She also ran the kitchen that prepared hot food for the homeless. When a tidal wave struck the southern part of the country, she chaired a group that helped provide new homes.

"Whenever there was suffering, I was around to extend a helping hand. Whenever I read about someone in need, I tried to send help. I gave away much of my income in the form of scholarships to the poor." Early in the 1970s, she helped form self-help projects in which poor farmers were given seedlings. When they sold their first crop, they returned the cost of the seedlings to her. She also helped them form credit unions so they would not be dependent upon banks. "In the Philippines I am known as one who is always ready to help anyone who is in need."

By 1971, Charito felt that her time had come to enter politics. She chose to run for the office of Mayor of Quezon City, a position contested by two other candidates: the incumbent of eighteen years and another who was the official Marcos candidate. Both men spent large sums of money on the campaign, and while Charito could have matched their expenditures, she decided to run a modest campaign. "There was much corruption going on and candidates would pay voters to cast their ballots for them. But I told the voters, 'If you sell your votes, you cannot expect anyone to serve you since you have already been paid. But if you don't sell your votes, then the one that you elect will serve you. If I give you a contribution, the other candidates will give you more.' "

Charito lost the election. Many charged that there was fraudulent counting and that the election had been stolen from her.

Throughout the Philippines there were charges of pervasive official corruption. Faced with widespread anti-American sentiment, political and economic instability, and a spreading left-wing rebellion in the south, on September 21, 1972, President Marcos declared martial law. "I have ordered the breaking up of all criminal syndicates. I have ordered the arrest of those directly involved in the conspiracy to overthrow our duly constituted government by violence and subversion." The president commanded the armed forces "to maintain law and order throughout the Philippines, prevent or suppress all forms of lawless violence as well as any act of insurrection or rebellion and enforce all laws and decrees, orders and regulations promulgated by the President personally or upon the President's direction."

The effect of this proclamation was to suspend the Constitution and dissolve Congress. Under various presidential decrees that followed, universities were closed, labor strikes banned and union organizing forbidden, eighteen Manila daily newspapers shut down, all crimes against the public order (which ranged from vagrancy to treason) transferred from civil to military courts, the writ of habeas corpus suspended, and a new constitution passed legitimizing "constitutional authoritarianism."

According to the government's own estimates, nearly 30,000 people were detained in the first few weeks after the proclamation of martial law.

Many of those who opposed martial law gathered daily at Charito's house. "My home had always been open to people of all kinds of persuasions, so long as they were working for the good of the country. After martial law was declared, even more people came to my home to talk about the situation. Children would come, adults would come. Religious groups met there, all talking about the problems and possible solutions. For peasants, laborers, all sorts of people concerned with social reform, my home became a haven."

It did not surprise Charito that she had come to the government's attention. Early in 1973 while having lunch at the National Press Club with a friend, a politically active priest, the manager came to their table.

"Those gentlemen there," he said, nodding in the direction of two men in civilian clothes, "they are from the military and want to see both of you."

Charito and the priest went to them.

"Miss Planas," one of them said. "I know you very well. I respect you. We just want you to come along with us. But please, finish your lunch first."

Charito, the priest, and a journalist who was also lunching at the Press Club left with the police. They rode through Manila while the police looked for others wanted for questioning.

Finally, they were brought to Camp Aguinaldo, a major detention center. There the police asked her about several of her activities in the past few years, in particular about her trip to China.

"I went as part of a trade mission for the Chamber of Commerce," she told them. Charito suspected that they were really more concerned with her remarks after her return. When speaking to audiences, one point she often stressed was the way it seemed to her that China belonged to the Chinese and foreigners were merely visitors. She knew that this was a sensitive point for Marcos who had repealed laws curbing foreign ownership of land, businesses, and banks. American military personnel were highly visible, stationed at twenty-three U.S. bases throughout the country. In 1973, the Philippines received $281 million in aid from organizations such as the World Bank. The government's official policy was to encourage foreign investment.

Apparently, the police wanted to do nothing more than put Charito on notice that they were aware of her outspokenness and involvement with anti-martial law activities. Soon the investigation turned toward a discussion of Philippine politics in general. Charito explained her position. "President Marcos declared martial law because he was afraid of a communist takeover. But look at the people who've been arrested. Most of them have one thing in common, including me. Every one of us is anti-Marcos. But not one of us is a communist."

(Charito's contention that political prisoners were not terrorists or subversives was supported indirectly in a report by Amnesty International prepared in late 1975. The report noted that since the imposition of martial law the government had not established conclusively the legal culpability of a single individual in the central cases of alleged rebellion.)

Commenting upon her afternoon at Camp Aguinaldo, Charito said, "They treated me courteously during the questioning. I was a well-known person and they were not going to do otherwise." The priest and journalist were not as fortunate. They were both detained.

The investigation did not temper Charito's criticism. Civic groups continued to invite her to speak, and during the next several months she addressed many Rotary Clubs, Girl Scout troops, Red Cross groups, and the Chamber of Commerce. She used each occasion as a platform to express her opinions regarding military rule.

Once again she was summoned by the military. This time a general wanted to talk to her. At Camp Crame, another detention center that later received notoriety by being cited by Amnesty International for its systematic use of severe torture, the general made an offer.

"Miss Planas," he said. "We are willing to let you go, let you out of the country—provided you leave permanently."

Charito reacted strongly. "What an insult. I love the Philippines as much as you do. I plan to live and die here, nowhere else. I'd like to travel to other countries. But I'm not going to live anywhere else. This is my country."

Charito knew this might be her last opportunity to escape detention. She had no intention of stemming her political activities. If she stayed in the country, she might join thousands of other political detainees in Filipino prisons.

She was prepared for that eventuality and made an unusual request of the military. "If you arrest me, please do not come to my house very late at night. I'm always ready and prepared to be arrested. I don't mind. But I do care about my helpers. They will get nervous and upset. I care about the other people in my home. They will be inconvenienced by a late night arrest. If you want to arrest me, just call me up. I'll go. I'm always ready."

During the following months, Charito continued her work with the kindergartens and farmers; she continued to speak out against the government.

On October 3, 1973, at 10 P.M. she was at home, resting in her room. There was a loud knock on her bedroom door.

"This is a raid. We are raiding your house."

Everyone at Charito's home was placed under armed guard in the living room. The police went from room to room conducting a search. By midnight another contingent of soldiers arrived, bringing their number to over a hundred. Later, a general arrived. The search continued until nearly 3 A.M. When Charito arrived at police headquarters early the next morning, she found fifteen of her associates there. Simultaneously in various parts of the city while the police held Charito in her house, raids were carried out at the homes of employees of hers. After initial questioning, members of the group were separated and transferred to various army camps around Manila.

Charito was taken to an overcrowded prison where she was fingerprinted a dozen times. This was a temporary holding center that contained both political prisoners and criminals. That night she slept on the floor.

The following day she was moved to Camp Crame, where she was given a prison number. "We had to wait in crowded corridors. There were so many people in the hall that there was no room for chairs, so we had to stand. It was humiliating."

She slept on the floor again.

Many of the soldiers recognized Charito in the hallway. They were upset by her arrest.

"Why are you here? some asked. "We know you help people. Why are you here?"

"I've been arrested."

"You are a good person. Why have you been arrested?"

"They've given me a number. I don't know why. They say I'm a subversive, but they never say why."

One interrogator cried when he met her. He knew about her and her benevolent activities.

After several days she was transferred to Ipil Reception Center at Fort Bonifacio, a camp for political prisoners. There she joined 132 men and 32 women. Barbed wire separated the male and female sectors. The only contact men and women had with each other was at mealtime.

The camp guards ordered the prisoners to keep the grounds clean but they did not provide them with any cleaning implements. "We didn't have water or anything to clean with. Most of my companions were poor—workers, farmers, laborers—but I was well off. Whenever visitors came to the prison to see me, I told them what we needed and the next time they brought it for us. I managed to get a water hose, empty drums, and other things we needed. So we all started working on cleaning up the place. Our morale was boosted by keeping busy."

But Charito did not remain in Ipil Reception Center long. One evening she was told to report to office headquarters.

"Bring all your things with you."

"Why? What do you want?"

"Never mind. Just get everything."

She took some clothes and a radio which had been brought for her.

Then they blindfolded her.

"I felt like a thing—a thing just taken and placed somewhere. It was dehumanizing. If you are a human being, at least you're told where you're going. What's the use of not telling you? So the very moment I was blindfolded I was like a thing, something less than human."

They put Charito in a jeep and drove for about twenty minutes. "The jeep came to a halt and I heard a big gate being opened. Two men brought me in, guiding me, taking me over grass, then gravel. Suddenly we stopped and I heard another door being opened. Only then did they remove the blindfold."

Charito was now imprisoned, held without charges, confined to a three by three meter cell—alone, without visitors, without mail, unable to exercise or get fresh air. She was held incommunicado, completely cut off from the outside world.

"It was a dirty, dusty cell full of insects. Every morning white powder flaked from the ceiling. They brought me my food in the cell. This was solitary confinement. For two months I was confined to that cell."

Prison authorities allowed Charito to keep her radio in the cell. "Luckily I had a radio. I am so used to speaking; here I had no one to talk to. So I sang and danced with the music from the radio in order to entertain myself."

Charito petitioned the camp captain for permission to exercise. She was granted five minutes a day in the sun.

"The insects were awful. They were biting me all over. I was given writing equipment, although I couldn't write a letter to anyone. So I used to write to the camp commander. I wrote him several letters, calling his attention to the bugs. I told him that I needed extra screens and also cleaning equipment. There was no answer from him. So after several weeks I swept all the dead insects from the floor and placed them in an envelope. I sent it to him and that got a response." The commander visited Charito in her cell and assured her that he would do what he could. The cell was cleaned.

"It was very hot in the cell so I requested an electric fan. They didn't want to give it to me. I then wrote a 'term paper' for the commander about the use of electric fans, pointing out how little electricity they used. It wouldn't cost them anything extra since I would use it only sparingly." The commander was not persuaded.

Three months after her detention Charito received her first visitor. Her family and friends did not know where Charito had been taken, but at a party attended by the Secretary for National Defense, Juan Ponce Enrile, a friend of Charito's, asked him if he knew anything about her disappearance. Enrile told the friend where Charito was being held.

Charito asked her friend to let her family know where she was. Enrile allowed them to visit her. On their second visit they brought her a fan.

"I was never physically mistreated during solitary confinement. They didn't have to use physical torture. They tortured me and my family psychologically. You see, I had been delivering four to five speeches every day before they detained me. Suddenly I was cut off from everything. My family didn't know where I was. In solitary I had to keep myself sane. Aside from singing and dancing to the radio, I would follow every insect and swat it. It was a way of amusing myself.

"I tried to make the cell a little better. When my relatives came to visit I measured the window in the cell and ordered curtains to make the place a little more pleasant."

Before her detention, Charito had been scheduled for an operation. Although she requested that the military send a doctor to confirm her illness, the prison authorities ignored her. It took several weeks before a letter from her private physician convinced the military to examine her themselves. They confirmed her claim, and she was sent to a hospital.

After four months of solitary confinement, Charito was taken from prison.

Although she was no longer is a prison camp, her detention was not over. While recuperating at the hospital, she was under constant armed guard. Only her family was allowed to visit. Secretary Enrile conceded to Charito's father's petition not to return her to solitary confinement. Instead, she went home under maximum security house arrest. Her home was under constant guard by sixteen soldiers, while two or three women soldiers took turns guarding her in her room. Charito was allowed no visitors, no telephone calls, and every letter she received was first screened by a military censor.

Three months later the conditions of house arrest were reduced to minimum security. Only four guards were posted at her home, and she could receive visitors with the military's permission.

Under mounting domestic and international criticism of his human rights violations, President Marcos agreed to release a number of prisoners who were being held without charge. Charito was among them. "The condition of that release was that we had to swear allegiance to the Constitution. I was willing to do that. In my mind, I was swearing allegiance to the old Constitution, not the new one. The new one was not legitimate."

In December 1974, fourteen months after her arrest, Charito was free once more.

The military required that she report to them every Saturday, and in order to leave Manila she had to request their permission.

"I'm single, but I used to joke that now I was married to the military."

The weekly reports lasted about five months before they were reduced to monthly visits, then one every other month.

"Every time I reported to the military I talked to them like a mother to a son. I told them about the situation in the country.

"I asked them why they were fighting for Marcos. I said, 'These people are getting richer every day. The situation will get worse here, and those people already have properties all over the world. They won't have to stay. You will be left alone to kill your own compatriots. And these people you are torturing love our country. They are intelligent people, just like yourselves. They are scientists, mathematicians. What will happen if you kill all the cream of the youth? What will happen when all that is left behind is the scum, the vicious ones?' "

"Please, Miss Planas," one soldier said to her, "don't generalize about the army. Not all of us are dishonest and brutal. Some of us know the situation. But we are in the army and have to follow orders."

Charito continued to speak out against the Marcos government. She was elected Director of the Chamber of Commerce. This provided her with the opportunity to speak throughout the country.

During one Saturday visit she was told that there was strong pressure to return her to prison. The government suspected that she was one of the prime organizers of the May 1 labor demonstration. Other times she was warned that her arrest was imminent.

Concern about human rights violations in the Philippines continued to grow. In a report issued early in 1976, Amnesty International had reached the conclusion that "torture was used freely and with extreme cruelty, often over long periods. In particular, torture was used systematically against those who had no means of appeal to influential friends or established institutions." President Marcos corroborated this claim when, in a televised interview in Manila on October 15, 1976, he announced that about 2,700 military personnel had been disciplined for maltreating prisoners.

In an attempt to bolster his country's image, President Marcos called for a World Peace Through Law Conference in Manila in August 1977. The *New York Times* reported that 2,000 people marched through Manila streets protesting alleged human rights abuses in the Philippines. The police used water cannons to break up the march.

President Marcos announced that he would soon call for elections to a newly-created National Assembly and would implement a policy of "restraint and compassion." In February 1978, Marcos announced the formation of the New Society Movement. He said he would not head his own ticket since the National Assembly automatically reserved a seat for him regardless of the election outcome. Instead Imelda Marcos was selected to head the party.

"Soon after Marcos made that announcement, I received a call from one of the opposition leaders asking me if I was willing to offer myself as a candidate. I told him that I thought that the election should be boycotted. I thought we should tell the people not to register and not to vote to show our dissent. To run in the election would be to legitimize it."

The counter-argument was that the opposition needed a forum to openly convey their criticism of the government. This would give them a visible platform by which they could inform not only Filipinos but the world about the situation in the country.

"He convinced me. I knew that it might be dangerous to run, and I was sure that I would be arrested again. But we started to form a line-up of candidates, and someone was needed to run against Imelda Marcos. A man couldn't run against her. When he

criticized her it would appear ungentlemanly. They needed a woman, so I was the candidate."

In the weeks before the election, Marcos increased government
pensions by 12 percent and teachers' salaries by 20 percent and
promised to reduce the price of slum dwellers' land from $83 per
square yard to 83 cents. Despite these concessions, the opposition's popularity continued to grow, culminating on the eve of the
election with a noise blitz: hundreds of thousands gathered in
Manila streets honking horns, banging pots, setting off fire-
works, and shouting anti-government slogans.

"We knew we wouldn't be allowed to win. But in the days before the balloting when all those people came to hear us, that's
when we won. We knew that Marcos had promised that he would
allow the people to vote. But he never promised that the votes
would be counted."

Fox Butterfield, the *New York Times* reporter in Manila at the
time, wrote,

> When this correspondent walked in on the [tally coun-
> ters,] they tried to cover up the rough brown-colored tally
> sheet and called for three guards who seized me and pushed
> me down the stairs.
>
> One of the tally sheets showed all the votes had been cast
> for the Government party and none for the opposition. No
> People's Force poll watchers were present in the school, and
> an angry crowd outside charged that the opposition's ob-
> servers had been thrown out early in the day by the local
> police.

Early in the evening on election day Charito received reports
from Laban coordinators that there were irregularities in the
counting. She went to supervise the tally.

"Later that night I planned to return home and wait to be arrested. But when I pulled up to my house, I saw the army already
there. They had surrounded the place. Although I was prepared
to be arrested, I decided at that time that they weren't going to
arrest me again. It is one thing to sit home and wait for them; it is
another to walk up to them to get arrested. I saw there was a
chance to escape."

Charito drove to a friend's house and that night watched the election returns on television. In addition to learning that the election counting was proceding very slowly, she heard that the government was looking for her. She was accused of harboring dissidents and hiding soldiers of the National People's Army. They claimed that she was a communist and subversive and offered as proof the claim that they had found a rifle on her bed.

"Marcos is such a bad liar. What kind of revolutionary would I be with one rifle?"

In a nationally televised press conference the next day, Marcos said that "undoubtedly the subversives have infiltrated Laban." He warned that the police would stem potentially violent protests and repeated that the police were still looking for Miss Planas.

On Sunday more than six hundred people were arrested while protesting alleged voting fraud and martial law. Four National Assembly candidates from Laban were among those arrested.

On Monday an official report of a presidential cabinet session stated that President Marcos was cancelling an order allowing "free debate and discussion of issues." It further warned that the President was determined to take "preventive and pre-emptive" action against dissent.

Later in the week Marcos claimed that the demonstration had been led by subversives and people under the influence of drugs. He claimed that the political opposition had engaged in "paying the voters and bribing poll watchers." He also announced that he was releasing nearly all of the six hundred arrested in Sunday's demonstration. Remaining in custody were eight leaders of the march, including the Laban candidates.

Charito listened to this news as she moved from one hiding place to another. Most of the time she slept on floors, but on several nights, while being hidden in warehouses, she slept on top of soda bottles. "On one occasion I was brought to a room and told to keep quiet, not to make a move so that the people outside wouldn't know that the room was occupied. When someone would knock, I would hold my breath. When nature called, it was a good thing I saw a basin."

While in hiding she developed a toothache, causing her face to swell. This allowed her to take on an effective disguise. She assumed an alias and with the help of friends she was smuggled out of the country. She was granted an American visa and arrived in the United States in June 1978.

"When you are detained there are two things that can happen to you. You either give up your commitment or you strengthen it. There is no other way. Once your commitment is strengthened it becomes part of you. Even if there is danger that you will be liquidated, you accept that as part of life."

Eduardo and Natasha Becerra

Chile

No one shall be subjected to arbitrary arrest, detention or exile.
*Article 9, Universal Declaration
of Human Rights*

*Although Chile was one of Latin America's leading examples
of democratic government, since the 1930s many Chileans recognized the need for social and economic reform. Reforms in these
areas were undertaken by Eduardo Frei Montalva when he assumed the presidency in 1964. Although he initiated social programs and began the nationalization of foreign-owned mining in-
terests, criticism of his government continued to mount from the
left.*

*During the 1970 presidential campaign, Salvador Allende, a
Marxist, campaigned on a platform calling for the expropriation
of foreign businesses. Garnering a one-third plurality of the vote,
Allende assumed office.*

*International lending institutions withheld credit, the country
suffered an economic blockade, and the economy began to dete-
riorate. The inflation rate soared past 300 percent, new ma-*

*chinery and machine parts could not be bought, the transporta-
tion system experienced dislocations, and there were food short-
ages throughout the country.*

*In the late summer of 1973, a military junta seized power in a
coup taking thousands of lives, including that of Allende. During
the next several years the junta was cited by many international
organizations for its policy of political arrests and torture. A
statement issued by the Conference of Chilean Bishops in 1977
noted that since the coup more than 900 political prisoners had
disappeared.*

BARELY ABLE TO contain her loathing, Natasha Becerra said to
the base commander at Antefagasto, "You have a patch of
gray hair now. I hope your head doesn't turn completely white
soon. You know what you are doing is something awful."

Eduardo, her husband, had just been informed that an order
had arrived from the junta in Santiago; he had been dismissed
from the Air Force. All his records, as head of the base artillery
unit, were seized; he turned in his officer's uniforms and his
weapons were taken from him.

Eduardo and Natasha would recall vividly an announcement
made several days later by the junta. In a public statement the
junta declared that they were going to rid Chile of all the "bad
herbs" and kill five million Chileans if they had to. But that
morning, September 12, 1973, one day after the coup, the couple
had no idea what lay ahead. They only knew that after years of
loyal military service they were abruptly returned to civilian life
and dismissed from the base.

No charges were leveled against the Becerras, but they could
easily surmise the reasons behind the dismissal. During the Allende administration, they often found themselves to be Allende's
only supporters on the base. Some of the right-wing officers attempted to engage Eduardo in political discussions, which
Eduardo always tried to avoid. Eduardo's interest in government
was as a concerned citizen, not as an ideologue. Natasha, too,
tried to avoid political discussions with the officers' wives. However, by the few things they did say and by their lack of vocal
opposition to Allende's policies, everyone knew that they at least
sympathized with the socialist government. Since Eduardo had

access to many of the base armaments, the leaders of the coup wanted him out of the way.

Only later would Natasha and Eduardo learn how threatened the junta felt and to what extent they would be defined as enemies of the people.

Natasha and their two children, Marisol and Eduardo, along with whatever could be packed into crates, left on a cargo plane for Santiago, while Eduardo drove the 1,400 kilometers south through desert country. They planned to meet at their cottage house by the sea near Santiago.

"One of my sisters came to the airport to meet us. In order to get to our house we had to drive through the city. It was terrible to see what was going on. We hadn't witnessed anything like this in Antefagasto because the violence was in the city, not on the base. Here I saw streets full of armed soldiers. I had never seen anything like it before. This sort of thing was unthinkable. You could say that up until then we were innocents, like little birds in a way."

For the first time, Natasha began to fear for Eduardo. Although he had special permission to travel, it was dangerous for him to be on the road, especially at night. She could not sleep until he arrived at about 3:00 A.M.

Their cottage was too small for the family, so the children were sent to relatives nearby. Eduardo drove back to the air base in Santiago to collect their belongings.

"I knew the commander there; we used to be friends. But when I arrived to talk to him, it was as though he had forgotten everything about our friendship. He told me I had two hours to get everything off the base or he would have it thrown out as garbage."

The Becerras lived in near isolation at their cottage. Their only neighbor was Natasha's aunt. They had no newspapers, and all the news they received came from the state-controlled radio station. They had little money since they no longer had an income and their assets had been frozen. They planted a vegetable garden and each day Eduardo went to the beach to fish. Every week Eduardo drove to visit the children at his mother's house and returned with some food to tide him and his wife over.

On the afternoon of November 7, after a hot day in the garden, Eduardo returned to the house to shower. Natasha and her aunt were chatting when they saw a man in civilian clothes crossing the lawn toward the house. Natasha demanded to know who he was and berated him for entering their property. He wanted to know where he could find Eduardo.

At this moment Natasha noticed a large revolver on his hip. On the road a group of men waited beside a car and beyond them were soldiers armed with automatic weapons.

She invited the man to wait for her husband in the house. Eduardo was informed that the Ministry of Defense had ordered his arrest. They accused him of keeping arms.

Natasha's temper flared again and she demanded to know where they were taking him since she was going also. The officer told her she could follow in her car if she chose.

At the police station Eduardo was transferred to another vehicle. Natasha tried to follow in her car, but she lost them as the car sped away.

That night Natasha thought about the summary executions taking place daily throughout the country.

"There were all sorts of sad and terrible stories those days. Even if you thought you were safe, that you had no connection with the Allende government, that you had nothing to do with politics, it wasn't very important. If they thought you were undesirable, that was enough. If they thought you disagreed in any way with the junta, that was all that mattered to them."

In prison in Santiago the next morning, after his name and other information were recorded, Eduardo was taken to another car.

"I was wearing a jacket and one of the investigators suggested I take it off. Suddenly, someone threw it over my head. I couldn't see. Then they shoved me into the back of the car where I was put between two people. One of them hit me on the side of the head. They called me a son of a bitch and told me not to move again."

Eduardo knew Santiago well and even with his jacket over his head he knew that they were not taking him to the Ministry of Defense. He protested and insisted that he see the Air Force Judge Advocate. They punched him again, warning him to remain silent.

"I used all my senses to try to figure out where they were taking me. I listened very carefully to the city noises, to the feel of the road. I figured out they were taking me to the Air Force's War College."

Once there they replaced his jacket with a hood. No one said a word to him for several hours. He could hear guards talking and a radio playing. There were occasional shouts from the hallway, then shuffling, as though shoeless people were running by.

A guard told Eduardo that if he moved they had orders to shoot him.

"Because of my military training I was prepared for difficult physical situations. Night came. It was very quiet. It sounded like a cot had been brought into the room and some people lay down. But I wasn't given anything. I stood all night. I calculate that I was there for three days, in one place, with a hood over me. They allowed me to sit only in order to eat. That was very difficult because my knees were stiff. I could not sleep during this time either. When they fed me, they lifted the hood only enough for me to see the dish under my nose."

Natasha began to search for Eduardo. She moved in with her sister Vivian and her family in Santiago. She went to the air base to talk to a colonel she knew. He claimed no knowledge of Eduardo's whereabouts but took a message from her for her husband. She tried to engage a lawyer but couldn't find anyone who was willing to help her. She heard that Eduardo was at the Bureau of Investigation, and went there with some food for him; she was told that they knew nothing about him.

She returned to the colonel who, this time, assured her that Eduardo was safe. He told her that she could bring clothes and shaving equipment for him to the Ministry of Defense. She returned with a suitcase and package for Eduardo but he never received either.

"I waited some more. I was becoming mad with the uncertainty and not knowing anything about Eduardo's condition or whereabouts. Those were terrible days."

After three days of detention, Eduardo was taken to another room. They ordered him to undress. He demanded to see the proper military authorities and asked them to take him to a military area.

"I knew where I was, but I didn't want them to know that. They had gone through a lot of trouble to make sure I didn't know where I was. They would kill me if they thought I knew."

Eduardo grew frightened when he realized he was in a torture chamber. They put his clothes on a bench, tied his arms and legs which ached from the days of standing. When he tried to move his arm, a wire cut into his skin. They shouted at him. An electric shock was applied to his genitals. They beat him on the chest and legs with truncheons and subjected him to numerous karate blows. When he fainted, they revived him with smelling salts. They never removed the hood.

"They asked me questions. They wanted to know if I was familiar with this person or that. But it was torture because of my political leanings. They didn't want information."

The first session lasted a couple of hours.

The next day he was asked to sign a confession. He was now accused of planning to sabotage the base at Antefagasto. They wanted to know who was behind the plot. Eduardo gave them the names of his father and father-in-law. Both had died many years before. He hoped that this concocted confession would gain his release. However, after checking the information, the authorities accused him of wanting to make fools of them.

He was tortured again, every day for forty-one days.

When his hood was finally removed, he saw that his torturer was a former schoolmate, an officer who had also been stationed in Antefagasto, whose wife knew Natasha, and whose children played with Marisol and Eduardo.

Eduardo was taken to Antefagasto to stand trial for treason.

During the time in which Eduardo was being tortured, the police arrested Natasha's sister Vivian at her house. Natasha had not been home that night. The following morning Natasha went to the Bureau of Investigation to inquire about Vivian. She entered a huge waiting room filled with people. There she saw her sister and, in happiness, her sister called to her. The police officer next to Vivian asked Natasha to give her full name. He informed her that she too was under arrest and that Eduardo had been returned to Antefagasto.

"A handsome officer, well-shaven and smelling from fresh cologne, put us in a van. They put blindfolds on us and then hoods. Someone took my arm and with a very kind, tender voice said, 'Please, madam, take care. Now we are going down some steps, then we're going up. Be careful.' Finally, I was seated in front of a small table. The only thing that concerned me at that moment was whether or not Vivian was with me. So I cleared my throat to make some noise. She did the same. I whispered to her to ask how she was. Someone told me to keep quiet. I could hear the sound of rifles."

First Vivian was taken from the room, then Natasha. They pushed her onto a wooden bench, exposed her breasts, tied her legs apart and began administering electric shocks. Her arms and legs twitched from the current.

"I was really scared. I thought they would kill us. I've always been afraid of electricity, ever since I was a little girl. I was terrified."

The interrogators told her that her children would not be safe.

"They asked me stupid questions, sometimes shouting, sometimes cursing. Some men would be polite, but then they would use the shock again, burning my breasts, putting it between my legs."

Although she seethed with anger, Natasha held her temper. An hour and a half later, as they led her back to another room, she said to them, "I've lived with the military for fifteen years. I've learned to like them and respect them. Now you. In one moment you are destroying all those things."

In the bathroom she reached for water. A young guard motioned to her not to take the water. She learned later that was a small act of kindness, as water in the body would only increase her pain.

In a van, on the way to another building, Natasha and Vivian sat next to each other, holding hands. The blindfolds were removed and they were allowed to call their family. An aunt came later with a blanket for the night.

They were held in that jail for two days, sharing the cell with two other women, being permitted to leave only for meals. They were then flown to Antefagasto. Natasha noticed that the pilot was a neighbor from the base. Natasha also recognized some of the military personnel at the airport. One officer in particular looked uncomfortable. Natasha singled him out, said hello to him, and inquired about his wife.

They were brought to a convent which, while being used as a women's detention center, also had nuns present. They ate their meals with the nuns, and on Sunday Vivian's husband came to visit.

But on Monday they were taken for questioning and were blindfolded again. They were now accused of espionage, claiming that Natasha had sent military secrets to Vivian. They said they intended to shoot Eduardo.

"I was so scared but I was also angry and the next minute I wanted to laugh because this was so stupid. I was afraid they were going to torture me again. I didn't know how long I could stand it. Maybe I would break down and admit things that weren't true."

They wanted her to confess to being a socialist. She said she did not belong to any political party. She said that she only had human feelings and was a humanitarian.

"I wanted to take the hood off. This was unbelievable, to confess to being a good human being meant that you belong to the left."

They threatened to shoot Eduardo if she did not confess, but she insisted that she had nothing to confess.

Hours later, in a room with Vivian, she heard Eduardo's voice coming from another room.

"They used many strange techniques. Maybe this was one of them, to let me know that he was still alive so I would make a confession. But suddenly I was full of strength again. Later they took me to another place where I could hear a man giving a confession. They wanted me to think this was Eduardo. But I lived with my husband for seventeen years and I knew he wouldn't do something like that. I had nothing to give them but from that time on I wouldn't have given them anything even if I had something to confess."

Later that day Vivian and Natasha were given a statement to sign which stated that they had nothing to do with subversive activities. After Natasha demanded that they change some of the wording to make its meaning clearer, they both signed.

The two women were taken to the officer in charge. The officer asked what the matter was when he saw that Vivian was near collapse. Natasha said they had been tortured. The officer asked where and issued a sigh of relief when she said in Santiago. He warned them not to speak out against the junta and then apologized for having taken them so far from their children.

Natasha insisted that she have a chance to talk. She told the officer that she loved and respected her husband. She was proud of him because he was an honest officer. They were released. Outside, Vivian told Natasha she thought they were going to kill her when she defended Eduardo. Natasha had not been aware of how angry she had been.

"We walked the streets like drunkards, the smell in the cell had been so strong. A young man stopped us and offered us money. I told him I didn't know him and couldn't take the money. He said that he knew me, that I had been the only officer's wife who picked up hitchhikers between the city and the air base. The next day we found a lawyer in the city who was willing to defend Eduardo."

Natasha knew that Eduardo was in Antefagasto but she could not get permission to visit him. Eduardo could not see a lawyer either. Until his trial in April, he was held incommunicado. At the trial, he was found guilty of treason. Many officers at the trial expressed disappointment when the court ordered him to a life sentence instead of sentencing him to death. Eduardo was remanded to prison in Santiago. There on his cell door was written "Prisoner of War."

For the first time in nearly five months, Eduardo and Natasha could see each other again; they were allowed one half-hour visit per week.

Slowly, under mounting international criticism, the junta began releasing political prisoners. The junta declared that if a prisoner had a visa he could apply for a review of his case. Eduardo petitioned to have his sentence changed from life in prison to exile. Although he did not apply for it, in April 1976 he received an American visa. A year later, under the joint sponsorship of the Long Island Chile Project, Great Neck Human Rights Committee, and the Ethical Humanist Society of Long Island, the Becerras arrived in New York.

Eduardo and Natasha agree that they were among the lucky ones, that thousands suffered worse fates. They do not want others to feel sorry for them or even compassion, but they do want people to know what happened to them.

"Some day all of this must be written, not merely to tell how much people suffered but to make sure that future generations will not forget. For our country, for our people, for the people of the world, for the future—everyone must know.

"I think we kept sane and strong and continue to love life because we believe in human beings. Whenever I looked around me—when Eduardo was being held in secret, when I was being held—I always saw some smiling eyes, a hand, something that made me believe. We know that there are a few bad people, but there are also good people. You cannot let the bad few spoil everything.

"Life is good."